LOVE CALLS
and
ROUNDELAYS

A potpourri of poetry and photo art

by WYN

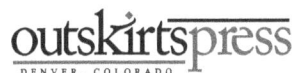

outskirtspress

DENVER, COLORADO

DEDICATION

This book is dedicated to my incomparable wife,
the spirit of music and dance,
and the power of Love.

Love Calls and Roundelays
A potpourri of poetry and photo art
All Rights Reserved.
Copyright © 2012 Wyn
v3.0

Cover Photo © 2012 Wyn. All rights reserved - used with permission.

Outskirts Press, Inc.
http://www.outskirtspress.com

Paperback ISBN: 978-1-4327-9769-0
Hardback ISBN: 978-1-4787-2017-1

Outskirts Press and the "OP" logo are trademarks belonging to Outskirts Press, Inc.

PRINTED IN THE UNITED STATES OF AMERICA

Contents - The Poems in This Collection

The Photos in This Collection

Gallery of Photo-Art

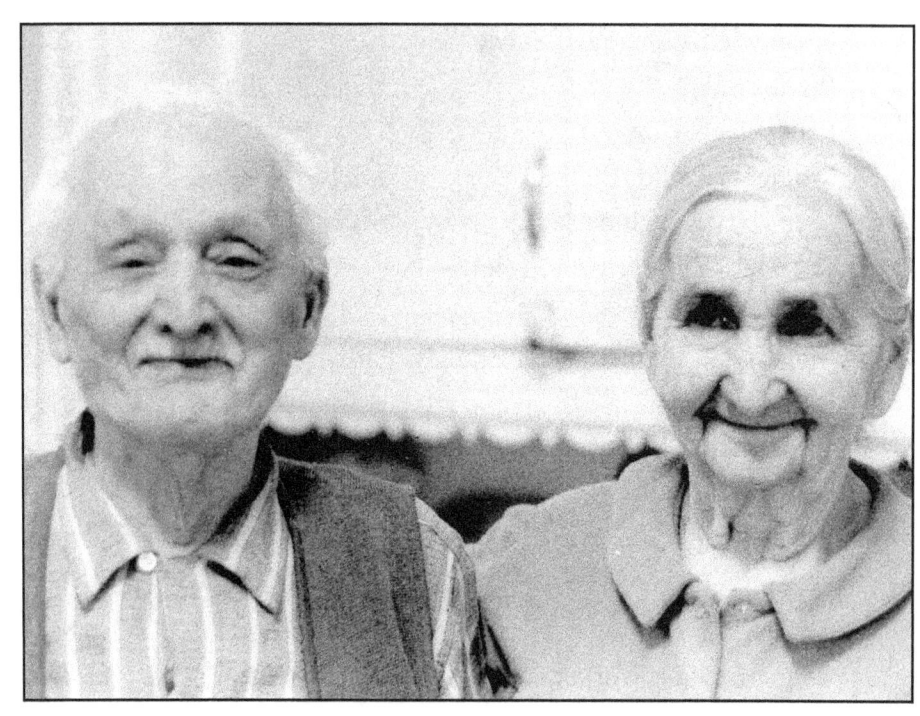

On Their 70th Anniversary

What is love?

What is love? Why so exalted, so relentlessly pursued?

Is love the heady nectar of the passion fruit
the afterglow of fervent nights
the sweetness of a lingering embrace?

Is love the pleasure of shared contempt
for all the fools around us
and their vulgar blatancies?

Is it a mirror of the ego's ever pressing need
for praise easily obtained through barter
by willful traders marking dross as gold?

Is love idolatrous or divine
a shrine a sanctuary escape
an anodyne that dulls life's cruelty and pain?

Is love the faith that somewhere
in this deaf-dumb universe there's one to hear
-and speak a siren promise of release?

Perhaps it's all these things and more
light bursts from an exploding star
an ancient comet's trail the big bang
beginning of another world?

An Epilove

and what is love grown old
if not a deeply valued concordat
twixt travelers on a worn out road?

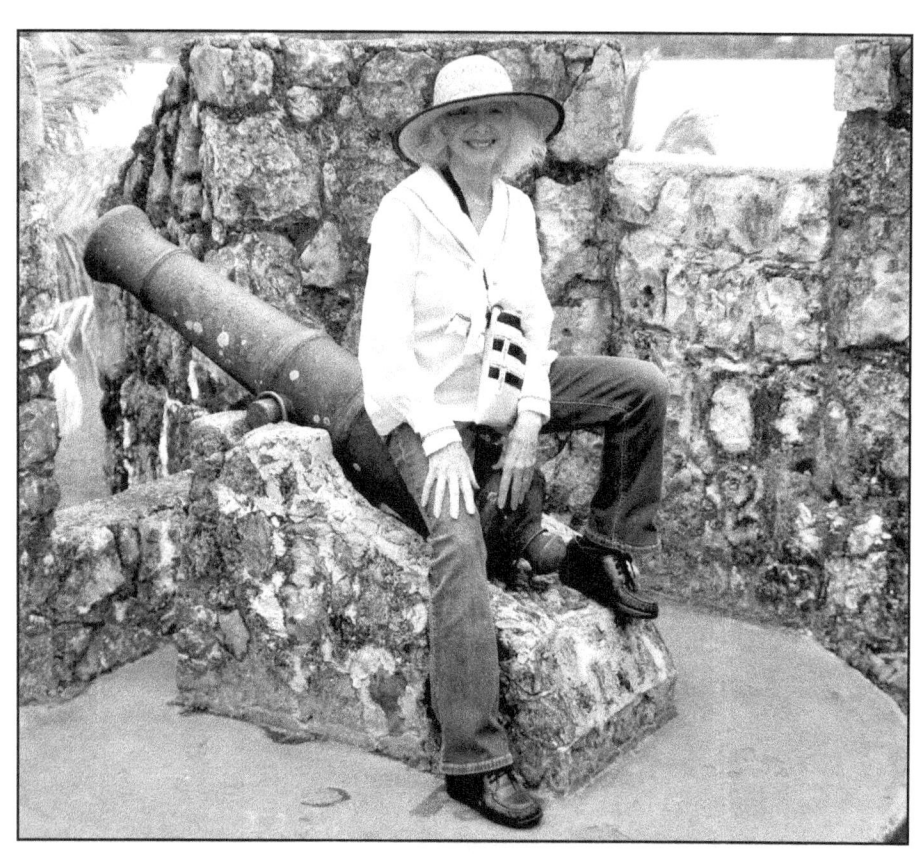

Milady at Fort Gun

To My Fair Lady On Her 75th

Here's a poem quite laborious
From a husband who's uxorious
A bosom bud, admiring scribe
who can't believe her years alive
amount to seventy and five.

What silliness! This cannot be
For surely blithe aerobic she
Is but a lass who out runs teens
And stuns men in her nifty jeans
My pride, my honey bee.

And though she often twits old me
And threatens in a hundred years to flee
It dissuades me not the least-est
For I love her best-est over all the rest-est
And always will.

And so you see love's labor's
Never lost!

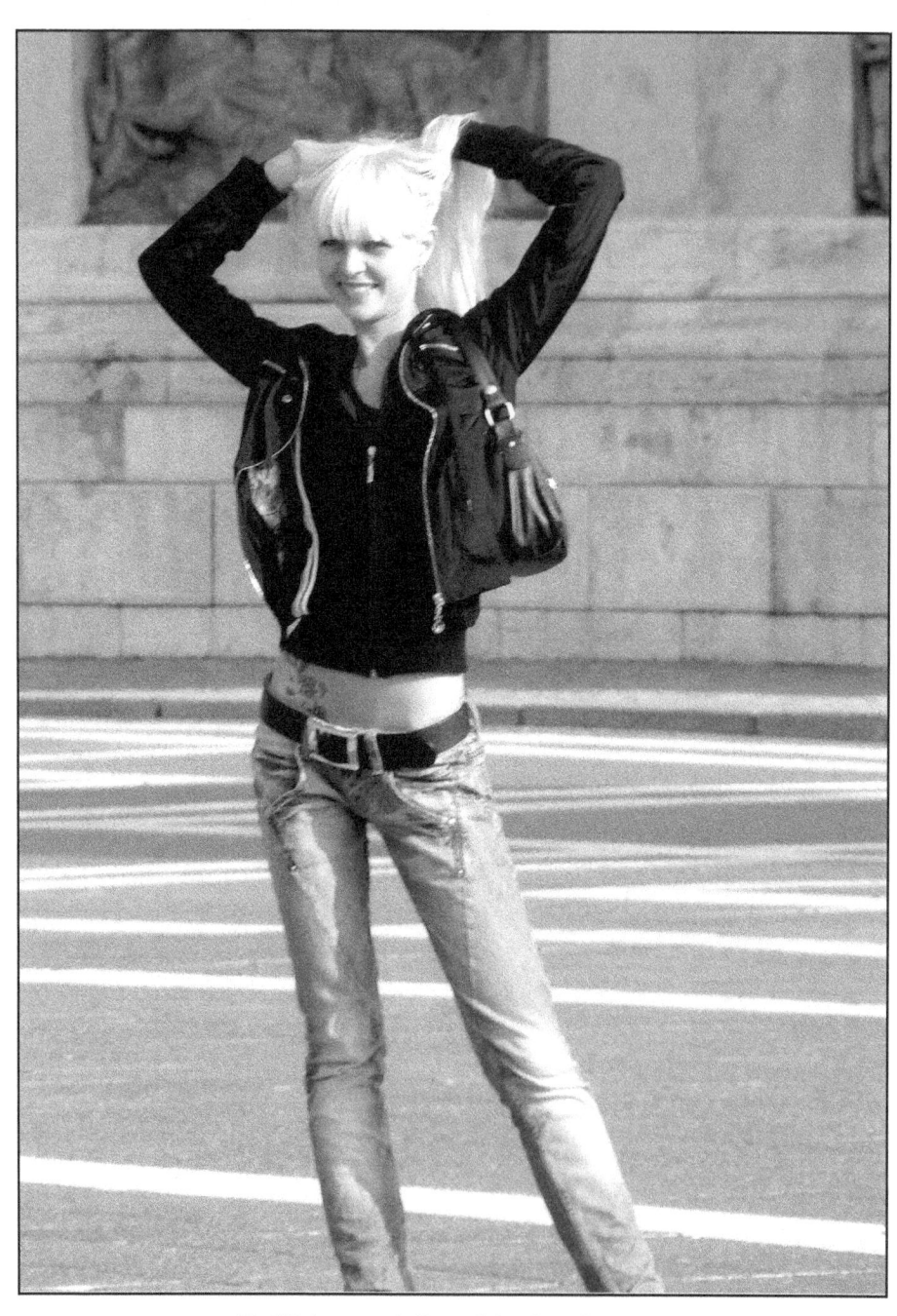

Bellisima – A Stand-in for Caralyn

To Caralyn - a budding actress

To say that she is fairest of the fair
Is fair enough yet not enough by far
To take full measure of this rising star
Whose beauty richly intertwined with art
Surpasses fair to capture mind and heart
Like some enchanted bird which soars on wings
of dreams, and sings of joy and pain and love
Inspiring poesy.

And so by jove,
though you and I may smile at this attempt.
at verse of praise and ardor whimsical
These paltry words hold truth enough to tell
inexorable time will shadow memory
and yet, I shan't forget fair Caralyn.

Starry Night

On such a night as this it seems
the bowl of heaven overflows with stars
whose bounty spills to earth
strewing my path with points of light
and though I know the little flashes
surrounding me in fields and woods
are only fireflies   my spirit says
I walk among the stars.

On such a night as this it seems
the stars are messengers of joy
the universe luminous and serene
and so for a moment I forget
that for each ray of light somewhere
there is a bolt of cruelty and pain
the Gods cast down to rouse us
from each pleasant dream.

On such a night as this, I remember
that we are all born of stars
that we all live by their light
and warmth as I my love
live by yours.

Fire On The Mountain

I saw it as I rounded the bend
fire on the mountain
demon beauty
a flaming path ascending to the top
and over it great whirls of smoke
an inferno
but no
delirious eye
intoxicated by a phantom
a narrow shaft of sunlight
stabbing across a dark mountain
overhung by billowy clouds
under a dusky sky
just a mirage
fire on the mountain
a mirage
burnt into memory.

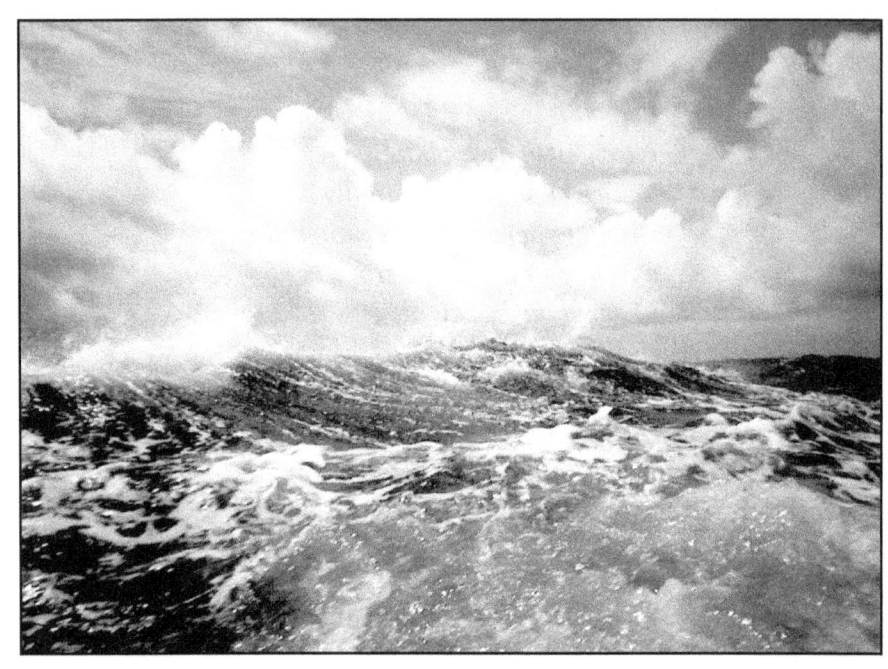

Sea and Sky

Ocean Song

In the sea, the undulating sea
waves hum mantras of serenity
let go, O weary one, let go.
See there in a calm grotto of the deep
the smiling Buddha lies
lips curled in loving peace
Nirvana.

In the sea, the siren sea
bare nymphs cavort and satyrs spree
rousing desire from restless sleep.
Awake, reveler, awake
light shimmers from a million stars
and watery spirits dance
a Bacchanal.

In the sea, the blood red sea
white sharks tear bellies of the bleeding whale
and in every dark abyss hideous sawtooths
grind and rend their living prey
obedient to eternal law.
Kill, hunter, kill
God's will be done.

In the sea, the sequin sea
where glistening treasures lie,
rich bounties gathered from the dawn of life
lure eye-probes of the mind
to abstruse depths.
Seek, hunter, seek
the antidote to pain and fear
in endless quest.

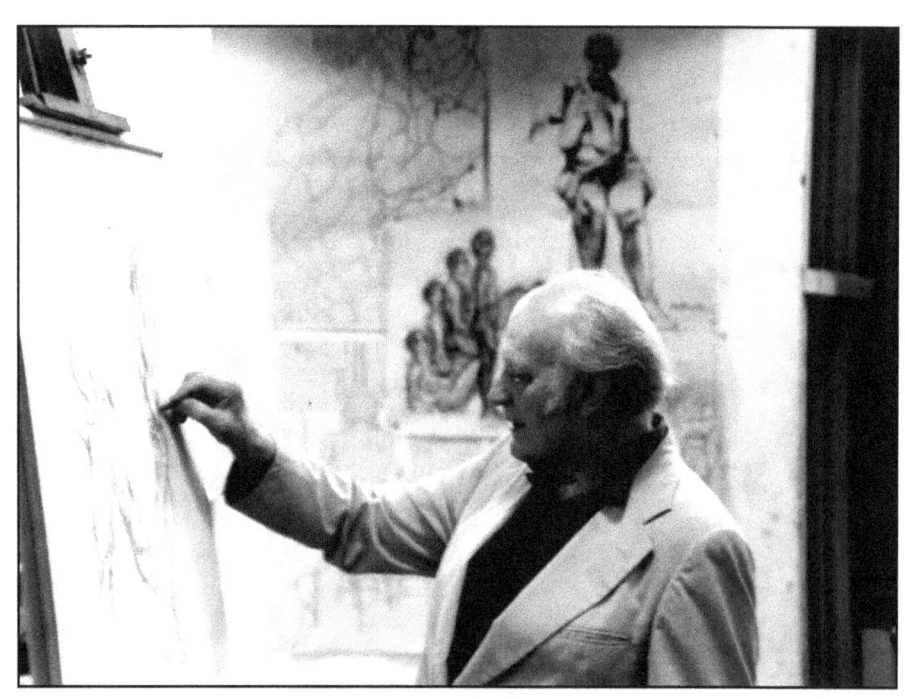

The Artist in His Studio

Art For Art's Sake

    In my studio, I dance with light
spirit aglow like Matisse in Morroco
or Monet at Giverny swimming in flowers
perfumes of hyacinth and lily everywhere
the scent of vinrose sunripened bodies
fever of the blood and brain
breathing life into my brushes
wetting them with joy.

    O my critic, spare me
your Mother Teresa judgments
your stupid censure endlessly prodding me
to open my art's window to the world's moan
to hurtful voices in the wind
and their ever rising cry: blood for blood!

    O moralist, servant of public commitment
to higher things you give your sweet-lip speech
then eat your fat dinner harvest dollars make love
while in the streets, the hate swells
like a gangrened arm and everywhere
the cry rises: blood for blood!

    Oh, tell me friend what can the artist do or you?
Did "Guernica" save Spain…or Hiroshima?
Did Jesus' love bar inquisitions
Or Marx end man's inhumanity to man?
Through all the sermons, hate swells like a bloated corpse
and everywhere the cry rises: blood for blood!

I'm here still in my moon-glow Giverny
gates shut, ears walled to the world's wail,
shuttered against hail storms of hate
and the ever rising cry: blood for blood!
Once more I dip my brush in the happiness
of flowers and rose breasts and all my love
for life and man is in my Art
for Art's sake.

A Poem Is...

A poem is diamond cut prose
shaped to a pointed arrow
sharp as winter wind
surprising as tomorrow.

A poem is mood distilled to essence
fire in the thermal brain
laughter in the womb
subtly profane.

A poem is rhythm of the blood
a caper at a conjurer's ball
where naked guests are garbed in light
and oracles enthrall.

A poem is word-dance to hidden music
graceful and free, an airborne pirouette
in which each turn slyly reveals
the mystery within...

A poem is the winged beat of myth
the claw of truth, the clamor of conviction
the spell of dreams turned into words
and words back into dreams again.

I Write, Therefore I Am.

I write therefore I am
reborn to rage at God
and weep or clown for man
made in His narcist image
nomad child of sand and stars
love-drunk in bedlam
hope shrunk to a consoling phrase

I write therefore I pretend to be
sooth-seeker with a lantern eye
hunter in labyrinths
as if my earnest quest
had healing grace
and thou O Ariel
could dissolve all pain...

Fallout

This poem is addressed to Bernadette Mayer, a poetry professor who encouraged me to poeticize with greater freedom, and especially with less concern about rules of rhyme and meter.

Let words tumble freely
from the thermal brain
fall-out of raunchy feelings
random quarks of pain
Can I do it
let it all hang out
forget rhythm
make rhyme tabu, sacre bleu
I'm starting to go wrong already
miss that beat that hidden music
can I dance without it
waltz my words around
un-honed unpolished
I'm trying Bernadette.

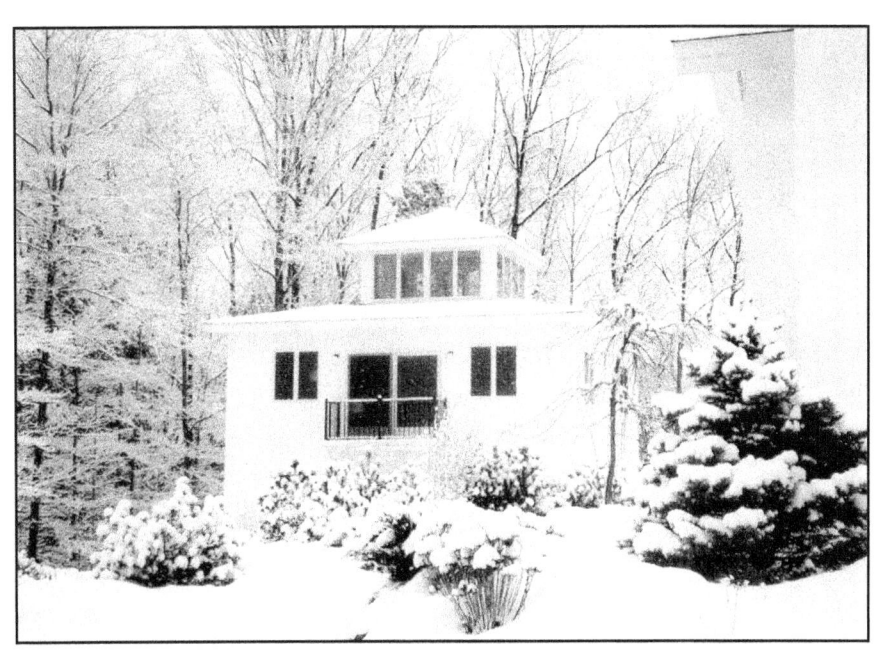

Winter Cottage

Wintersong

Who loves the winter loves with me
its chaste austerity
its crisp air, chilly peace
hibernating time
when the pearl black pond speaks silence
and vapors rise in the sharp cold air.

Who loves the winter loves with me
brisk waking hours
when snowy fields are crystal strewn
sparkling in the slanted morning light
and white brushed mountains stretch
across the quietude
their flowing silhouettes
pierced by straggly pines
and all about, tall oaks and maples
stand lean and leafless
finely branched in snowy filigree
and heavy-laden hemlocks
sentries to tranquility.

Who loves the winter loves with me
to walk the woodland path
under a gentle canopy of snow white
branches interlaced with sunbeams
Oh sacred arch of light
Oh white cathedral of the forest
envy of Sacre Coeur

Who loves the winter loves with me
its breathless serendipity
in each frozen instant of the rude outdoors
the wanderer's inner smile recalls
a fire's glow, warm shelter at the hearth.

First Touch of Spring

The last ice floe has melted on my pond
Its fresh swept surface now a beacon
Luring mallards to splash down
In landing fields of light
Windblown across the water's
Dappled darkness.

All earthen are the wooded fields
Yellowed by winter's debris
Trees still bare as if
The season's muted start
Were meant to mime late autumn
Grown old and sage and resonant
With half-toned harmonies.

Such shy impersonation cannot hide
Glint of white crocus, robin on the branch
The warm green spreading on the lawn
Briskness in the stroller's stride

Farewell you spirits winter worn
Welcome first touch of Spring!

Summer

Now is the time of brilliant days
love calls and roundelays and all
the heated stir of summer's alchemy.

See how the ardent sun woos fields to ripen
calling every bud to flower every weed to grow
firing the blood rousing the honey nectar
that draws the yellow-jacks and bees
to buzz each zinnia and rose

Here in the rich green mantled countryside
all nature glows the fallow deer stands proud
by ponds where mirrored swallows fly
and in the blossom scented breeze
new leaves sway lightly offering a tasty treat
to aphids beetles moles and mites
themselves a feast for hunter birds.

The craggy farmer toils in sprouting fields
where corn stalks bolt tomatoes clog the vine
fruit trees fruit and by the Buddleia bush
the butterflies perform a fairy dance
while in the starry theatre of the night
odd creatures merge their trilling melodies
to the deep gwonk sound of frogs
and the dze-dze cricket song.

Autumn Morning In Arcadia

As dawn lifts the shade of night
fingers of light play on my pond
its pearl grey waters framed all 'round
by irridescent fields of morning frost
Beside the little arching bridge
three crows peck at the teaming earth
and unseen creatures die that they may live.

Woods stir to the daily quest of deer and turkey
rustling like a breeze through dancing leaves
and lo, the sun rains down its golden beams
on orange red maples, birch, and evergreens
Behind the pond and fields, the mountains stretch
resplendent in the radiant hues of autumn.

Thus artful nature hides its ravening claw
concealing with sweet disguise its mordant law.

Winter Blues

There's a dreariness to winter
drab hours when rain turns snow to sleet
damp cold chills to the bone and
barren skies feed barren thoughts
aneurysm of wounded years
and injured centuries.

Can you help me lover-friend to drive away the winter blues?

There's a loneliness to winter
ice-numbed hours when my plodding eyes
peer out the window to a glacial field where
a lone horse stands stiffened by the cold
and I turn darkly away
in impotent dismay.

Can you help me lover-friend to drive away the winter blues?

There's a heaviness to winter
leaden hours when dusk casts shadow over day
and naked branches weave in disarray
stretching across empty skies
over impatient fields
yearning for rebirth.

Can you help me lover-friend to drive away the winter blues?

I will help you lover-friend dispel dark spirits of the heart.
I'll sing you songs of incandescent hues
warm notes to melt the boreal blues
I'll turn lights up for you in winter,
radiant lights to scatter gloomy grays.
I'll turn love up in winter, turn love
way up to drive away the blues.

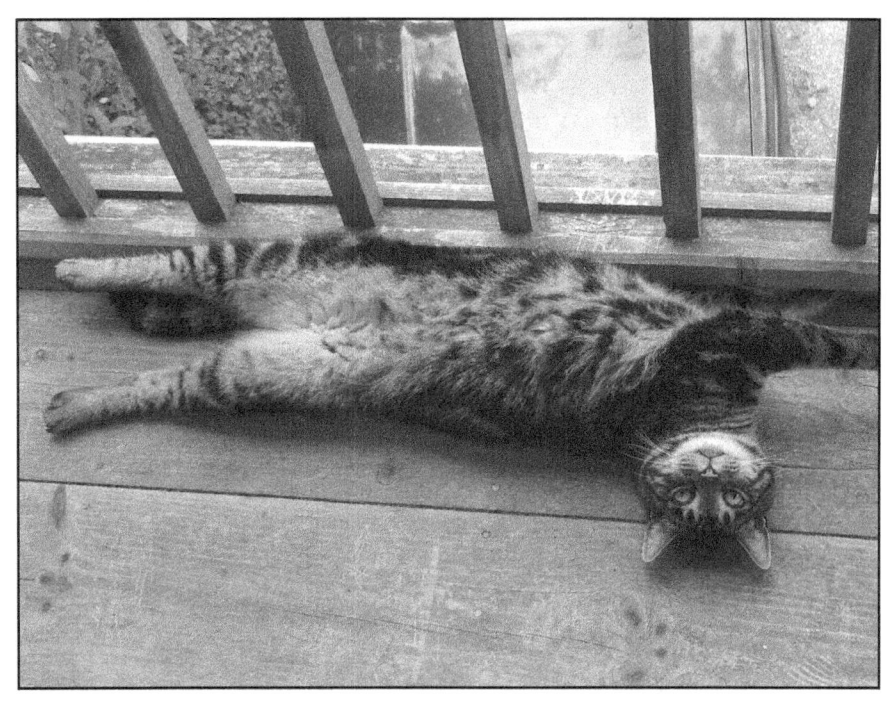

Stretch Cat

Hey Pretty Kitty
A Cat-atonic Lay

Hey pretty kitty, say
what's on your play-list for today
a pirouette, a tour jete,
a nap, a climb, a daring stray,
a lunge to capture little prey?

No winter gloom or stormy gray
can shoe your son'rous purr away
or mar your grooming self-content.
With lang'rous stretch and frolic fey,
you're numinous, divinely gay.

Pray tell me O cat, what magic is that
which dispels all despair and souci?
How I wish I could be as carefree as thee
Meow, pretty kitty, Ole!

A Pretty Kitty Postscript:

If you're a cat lover, you've doubtless marveled at the flowing grace of every feline movement. Perhaps you'll agree with me that all great art is imbued with the allure of the cat gesture.

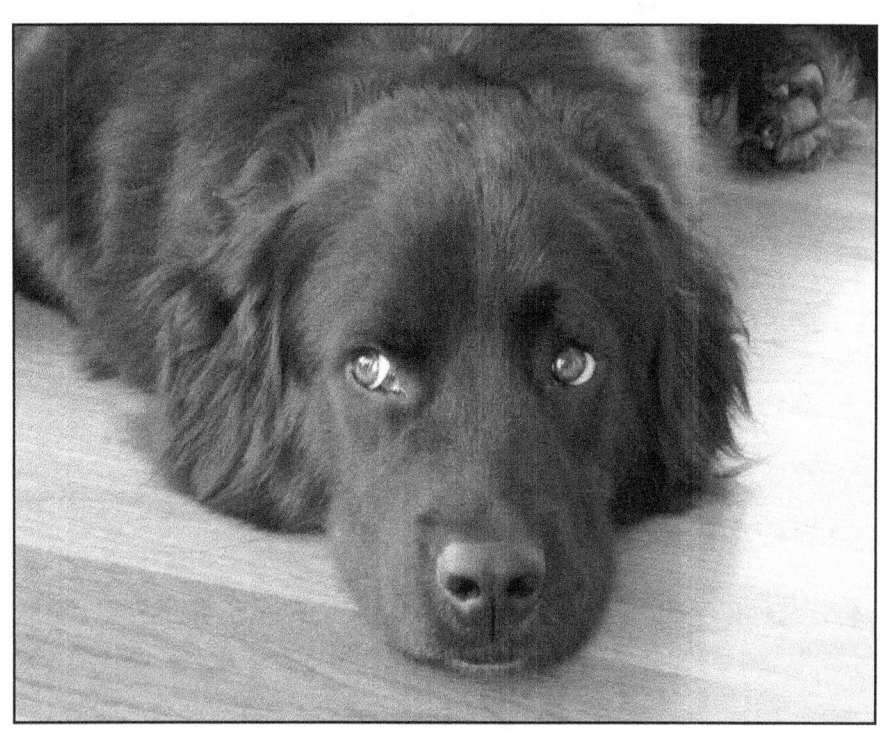

My Dog Shad

A Eulogy to Dogs

especially my dog Shad

I suppose that in the world somewhere
There is a dog as wunderbar as Shad
It's possible Could be,, I suppose,
since nothing's sure, I won't be
dog-matic. Still, I must say

when you look into Shad's dark
glowing eyes, you'll see a sensibility
deep as a coral sea
lovely as the Song of Songs
and full of meaning which
he valiantly conveys in

signs, lacking words to tell
Yet he seems content to loll
at my side, and when puss
runs round him pawing
now and then, Shad yawns
indifferent to female wiles
a Macho Dog, strong but

free of hate, free of sin
free of malice sapien.
no warrior except in play
yet I must say he's big, real big
on defense, and shows
fierce mandibles

so if you come to our door
in the wee hours of the night
unheralded, Beware of Shad
He'll eat you!

Renaissance Man

He's an interactive guy
with a global eye keyed to
speed on the info super-hi

revs with America On-line
is CAD-ish on design
logs on to Forex every day

a wiz on currency play big risk
big money off screen he's green
in cowboy boots and gabardine

married but unharried
safaried shot elephant and lion
with his N-90 rapid fire Nikon

white water rafted Land Rover-ed
to the Great Wall the Wailing Wall
Victoria Falls the Stamford Mall

hot for tutus and ballet
keen on Mozart Massenet
Da Vinci and Givenchy

favorite books are Free to Choose
Fountainhead and Future Shock
wary of commercial schlock

he's sunless tanned and lean
aerobic low cholesterolic
vita-tonic nonalcoholic

has drip painted a la Pollock
self published his own book of rhyme
amazingly he has the time

to do it all Hey tell me if you can
what's it all about
Renaissance Man?

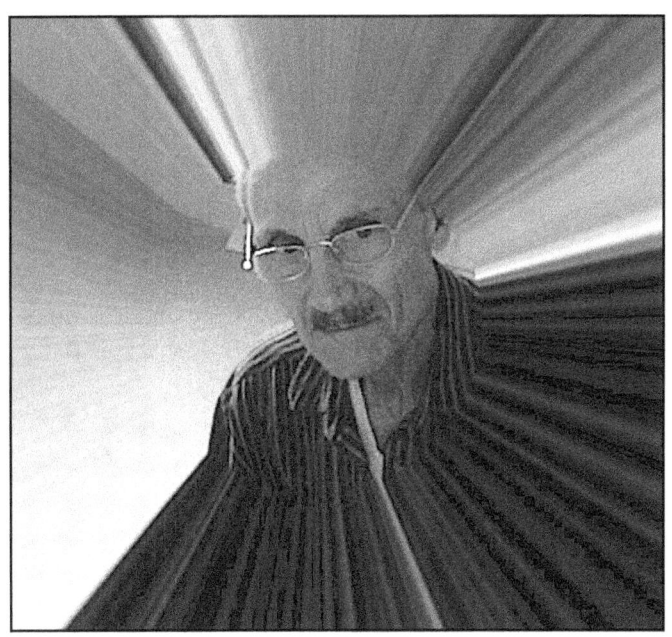

Ray Man

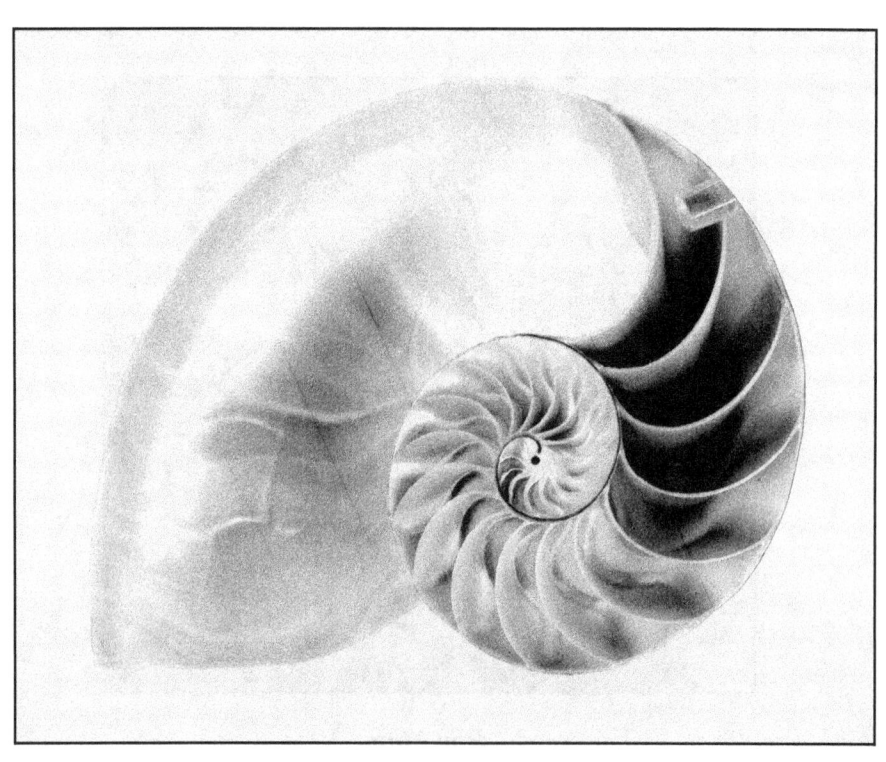

Chambered Nautilus

Ode To A Pearly Naut

O ancient mollusc of the Asian sea
I marvel at your aquability

life on the bottom doesn't get you down
you spread your tentacles and dine around

without psychic alarm you exercise
your copulatory arm or fraternize

with another cephalo-gal who though well bred
has grown her feely feet around her head

all that obtrudes two tiny pinhole eyes
much used to check out fishy passerbys

as need occurs, you build a larger home
slide in and deftly park your dorsal dome

without regret, you seal off out of mind
an arching shell of rooms you leave behind

with briny stir your sailor's life is fraught
what do you think it all will come to Naut?

An Advertisement:

God-On-Line'
(your Divine Connection)

Free Hook-up
Free Warm-up
Free G.O.L Tutorial

Try God-On-Line Now
Pay Later On our
Centennial Plan   You'll find

God talk really cheap your chance
to chat   chew the fat talk over
all you long for all that you lament

lost love?   feeble talent?   faded hope?
you can jibe or joke rant or wail
frankly   it won't matter at all

No other ear can overhear
no one can interfere
with your providential link

By Jove call now why wait
until you reach that Orphic gate
go man go get underway

connect direct with
God-On-Line.

Note: **we provide the divine connection**
no other warranty no refund for reticent reply

The Beat In Me

(An S-less onnet)

Ah pring is prung
lovebird burt into ong
time for a new tart
let me peak plainly
I've no kill to educe you
with my ex appeal
but I will onnetly reveal
my elf if that will end you
tho you deny me bli
I will not hi you
for I'd rather ki you
O you can wiftly ee
the beat in me is peaking.

A Child's Treat

- Have' A Carrot!

Want a nosh? Have a carrot.
That's no nosh.

Then have an apple or some cheese
another bite of cereal if you please.
That's no nosh either.

What's a nosh?
A nosh is a delish.

Is it a hamentash a knish
or maybe a fried fish?

Come on. Don't tease.
You know my favorite nosh
It's just a dish of ice cream
with lots of butterscotch
on top.

Now that's what I call a nosh!
Yum. Yum.

On The Campaign Trail*
(*on the eve of the Nov. '92 election)

The roundup's on, the dirt is flyin'
Who says old politics is dyin'?

George nails Bill the Bozo hard
and slyly calls Al's Ozone card

Slick Willy's saddle cry ne'er slips
from trickle down and read my lips

At dirty tricks, Ross cracks his whip
tags Bill a chicken, George a chip

while Danny lassos Murphy Brown
'cause Gennifer Flower's out of town

King Ron is back to help his friend
find big win issues at trail's end

It's almost over, boys – call it a day
Yippee- i- oh, Yippee- i– yay.

*A Note about this Poem and the Exciting Campaign of "92

Near its start, this poem refers to "George", i.e. - George H.W. Bush, and "Bill" also "Willy" for Bill Clinton. Later, it alludes to "Ross", that is to 3rd party candidate Ross Perot, and to "Al"Gore,the ardent environmentalist. "Danny" is the GOP's VP candidate Dan Quayle. One highlight of the lively polemics of '92 was an attack on Bush's "read my lips" pledge of no tax increase, later violated. More scatological was the charge that Clinton had an affair with Jennifer flowers, which of course was only the beginning of the allegations about Bill's amorou

Old

There it was somehow
unexpected yet hardly a surprise
suddenly old
suddenly bearing all the stigmata of age
the marks like tree rings
  counting wrinkled winters
  to oblivion.

A Toast to Laughing Gods

Shall I mourn the fallen leaf,
the broken limb, the dark abyss
of senseless space and time
that mocks each noble gesture
with an eternal yawn?

Ah well,
what use to moan the winter wind
when I've another spring or two
to sing with larks, play harlequin
and, with a wry conceit, drink
ambrosial toasts to foolish men
and laughing Gods.

Delirium

It's spread from lymph to liver the doctor says
so this is it. I ask myself what dying will be like
what pain what fear how I may choose my time
then in this brooding reverie I see her

> *Tutsi girl in a martyr's church cowering*
> *beneath her mother's still warm breast*
> *by the crossed window light eyes wide*
> *in frozen fear of the searching knives.*

O Child, dearly beloved child
   what is my fear to yours?

The pain has drilled into my bone and spread
to everywhere I watch it moving thru my moan
the needle comes ah true love blessed morphine
in my dazed relief I see the Tutsi girl again…

> *the whetted blades have found her*
> *they are hacking her upraised arms*
> *her face her pleading eyes*
> *slashing a cry to silence.*

O lamb of God
   what is my pain to yours?

I am still fighting for breath and meaning
a hand touches my last hours my wife I think
more agony more morphine I am choking again
swallowing a last pill in my delirium I see

> *by the crossed window light*
> *they've torn the girl apart*
> *wild dogs have come to chew*
> *her flesh and bone.*

O beloved child of everyman
   What is my death to yours?

> *Dies irae. Deus vult.*

Notes From The Underground

On sparking tracks the train wheels roll
in the great underground of the polyglot
stewpot New York New York
largest subway system anywhere
a thousand passengers a minute
flung together in the moving blender
of the city's mole cavern

Unhomogenized in all colors and flavors
Grundgy dissonant diversity on wheels
brou-ha-ha of surly underclass
a few blue collars many whites
a rouged brown in purple tights
next to a neat head-banded Japanese
gazing across the aisle to three boys
in sneakers punching each other
under a "save the children" ad.

From a corner shadow, a drug-eyed pony tail
casts star beams at an aureole face.
The winepress cars are full now
of close bodies distanced by thought
windows blink rapid fire at passing tunnel lights.
Against a side wall, a Charlie Chaplin man
is squeezed by bulging thighs.

Over the train's din, a cracked voice
mutters loudly to itself
too many people, too many people.

Night Chant

Do you hear the city
moaning in the night
oo-ow oo-ow oo-ow
piercing cry of the police car
fire engine ambulance
racing from pain to pain?

Do you hear Death
calling in the night
oo-ow oo-ow oo-ow
morgue music mournful
dirge to gunned down youth
and all the newly crucified?

Do you hear the world
wailing in the night
oo-ow oo-ow oo-ow
howling for the gutter child
the gaunt refugee
fleeing famine
and never ending war.

Do you hear the revelers
singing in the night
whoopee?

Obscenities

Twisting her curl casually
she told me she "got laid" last night
hard talk for me of nearly virgin birth.
I would have said "made love".
Such chaste refinement seems absurd
when violence screams in broken streets
and bloodied children die
each day from ethnic cleansing.

After centuries of carnage
who cares if words reek
odors of the fetid grave
hard rock hard cock macho mock
thrust of pretended power
defiant epithets
screw it all
turn up the arrogant amp
turn off Mozart till tomorrow.

To A Lost Friend

Looking out the window
I saw my favorite willow
waving in the wind
taller each day I swear
an airy graceful creature
like you my dear
this morning it was gone
all that remained
a little stump cut neatly
all 'round by ravening beaver teeth
small loss I'm told
another will grow to take its place
small loss (my enchantress)
but oh how pained I feel
how un-consoled.

Flood

We are inundated by images
why paint?

We are swamped by words
why write?

We are too many
why be?

There is plenty of time
to die,

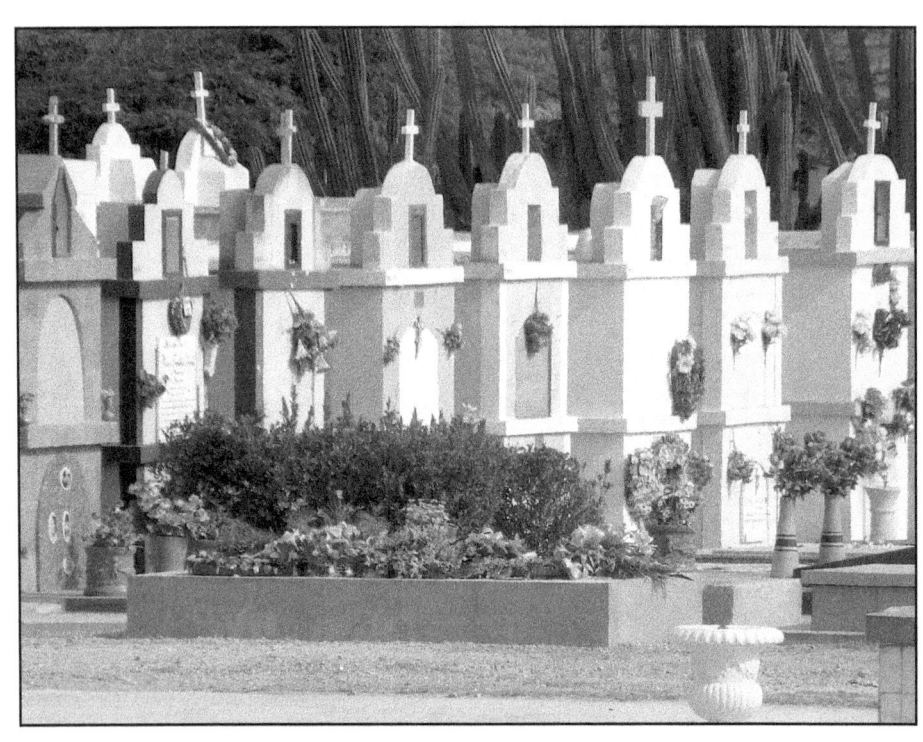

Grave Stones

Repeats

In the hurly-whirly space of the big-bang expanding
universe old stars implode black jaws gulp light
chaos keeps repeating repeating

Aloof the genome press goes right on printing
cryptic pages with a few odd letter changes
DNA just wants to keep repeating repeating

Man-copies each one resolutely seeking
to prove he differs by a meaning
each man strives and keeps repeating repeating

while the temple goers keep on chanting
mantras to the shattered beautitudes
folderol that keeps repeating repeating

Between the bitter requiems of mourning
for all the Golgothas and crystal nights
history just keeps repeating repeating

Perhaps 'till scribes of the second coming
rewrite flawed letters in the book of life
birthing a new man-child who won't

just keep repeating repeating...

All Writers Got The Blues

All writers got the blues
don't matter their color and stuff
or who they're foolin' with
or how much they weigh with their shoes off
'cause the bottom line is
they know what you are like
deep down
and
they're about the same.
which
makes 'em sad.

Nostalgia

Was it better when the universe was small
a little church where man and God
felt close not lost in infinite space
with only pulsars and quarky sparks
to light a soulless sea?

Was it better when innocents believed
most men were good and some
unblemished heroes
born to noble deeds
not prisoners of need?

Was it better when people trusting
in themselves and in their brothers
imagined they could build
a Shangri-La on earth?

Was it better before the mighty
greed machines gushed wealth enough
to satisfy all common wants
and inundate our dreams?

Stuff

Think of people dying every day
imagine all the stuff they leave behind

piled up unseen in attics basements barns
mountains of stuff enough

to fill a billion dumpsters shoes shades
tattered chairs rag dolls from country fairs

torn dungarees old paints and pills ladders
brushes drills war medals and stained flags

stacks of photos catalogues and books
bundles of Longevity and Life

Playboy Playgirl love letters unremembered
boxes of words boxes of used up forests

great heaps of words piled up past understanding
flowing over us like lava ash

of countless eruptions inundating time
* my God why am I writing this?*

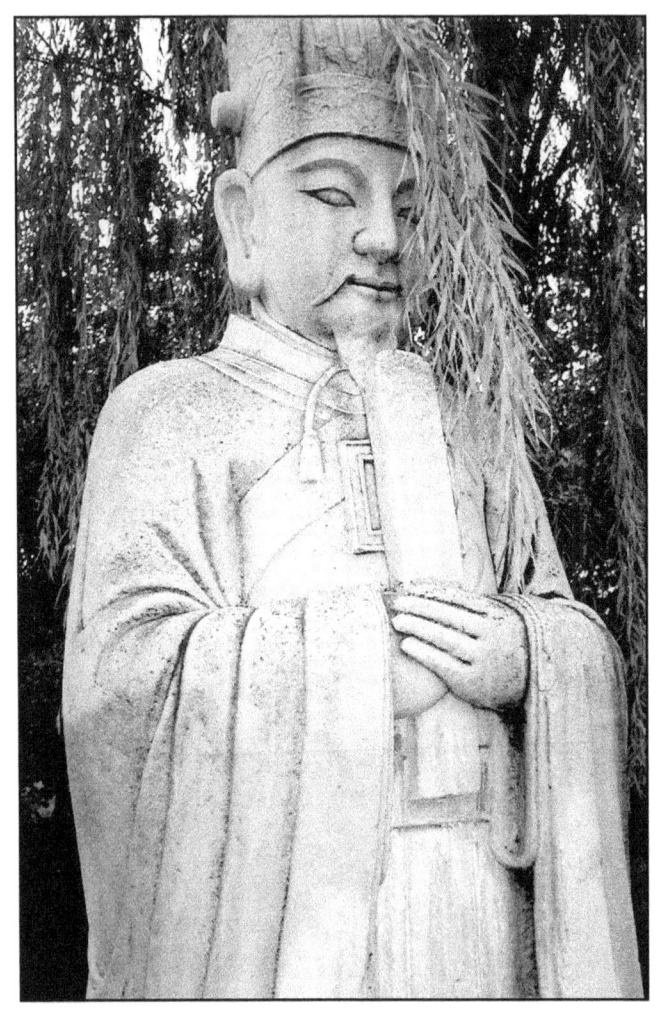

Sage statue

Sermon On Mount Tomorrow

He looked tall up there
standing on Mount Tomorrow
in my dream my little father
telling me his dream again
certain as always delivering
his sermon from on high
in his true believers words:

Up from a dark past, up I say
Up from the pain and helplessness
of hunger and disease
Up from the senseless strife of centuries
Up from venomous hate and chauvinist wars
and the era of short brutish lives
Up from carelessly contaminated earth
and brazen eulogies to greed
Up history's one rising stair
of growing knowledge
of Science wed to Art
to transform man
and bend space to new dreams.

On to the wonder of tomorrow!

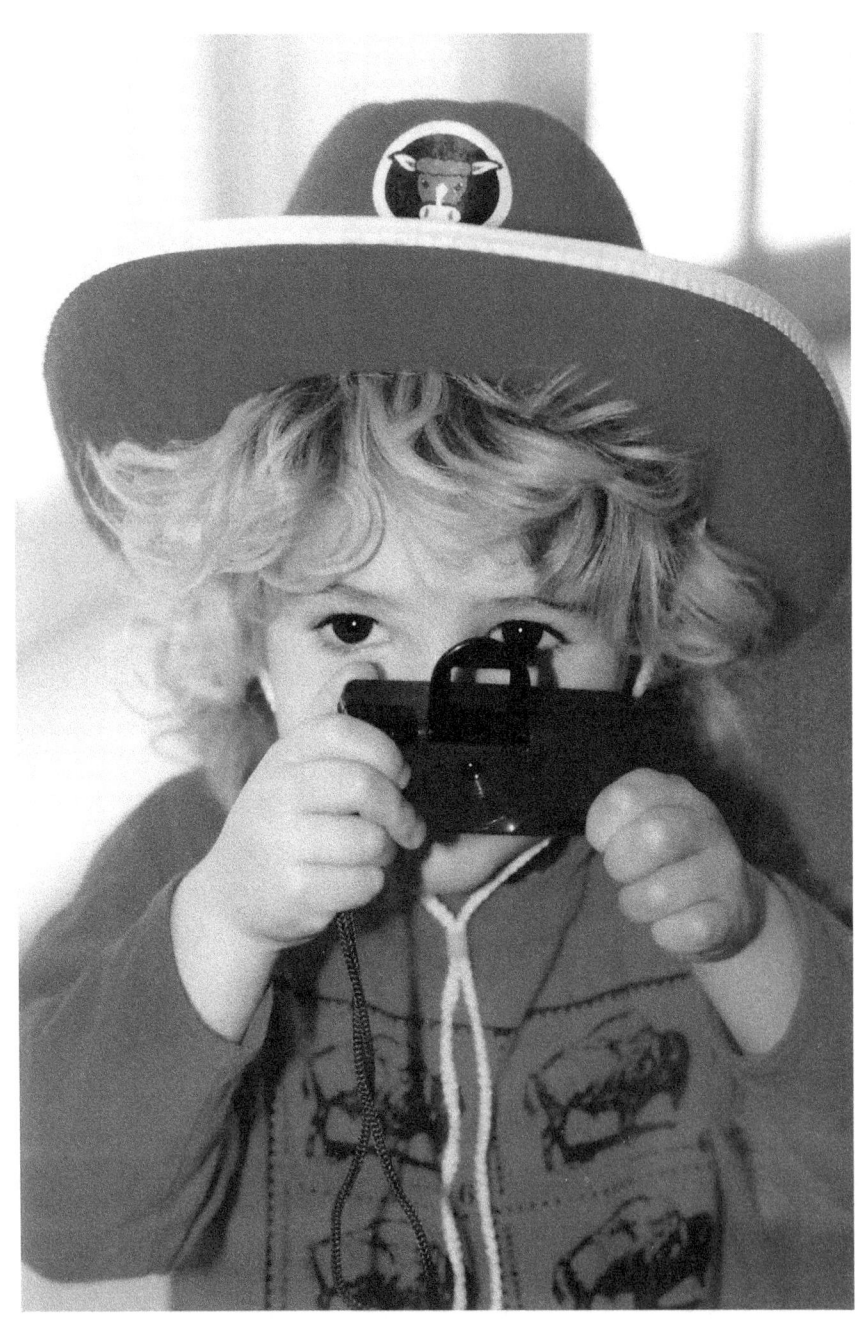

Sharpshooter

Gallery of Photo-Art   The Selective Eye

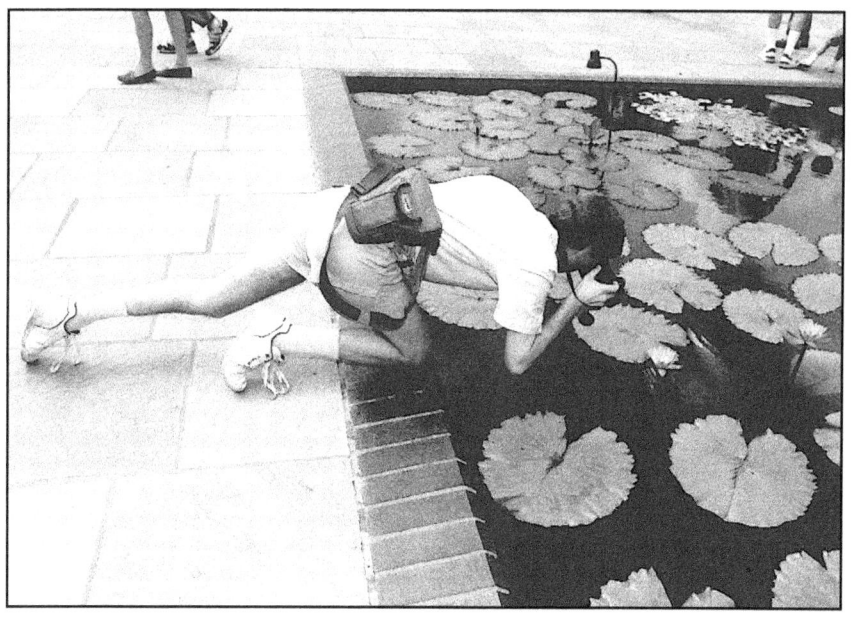

The Avid Photographer

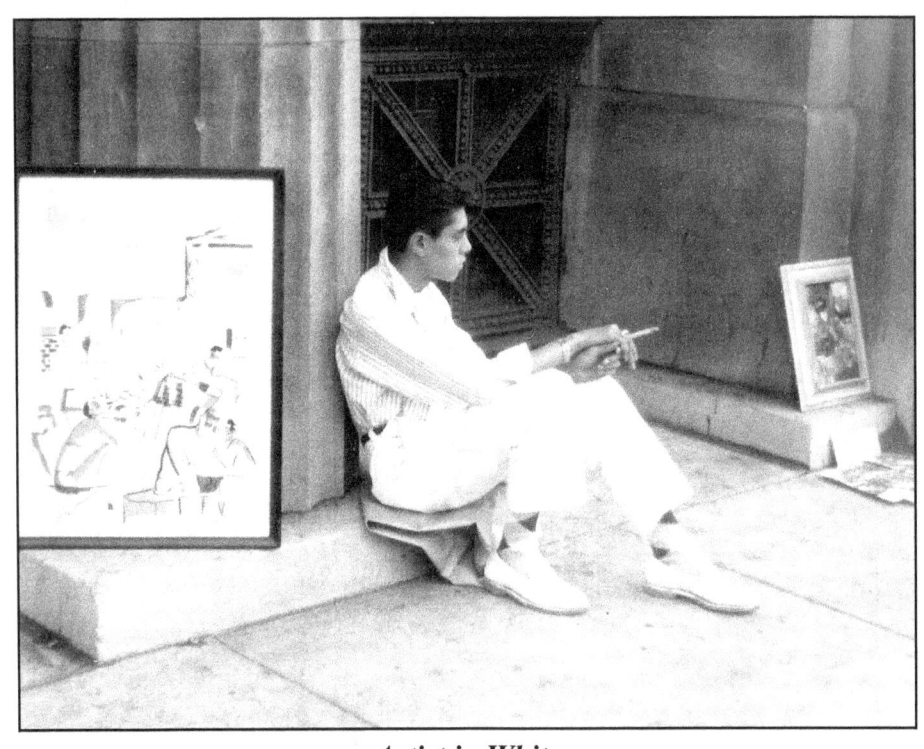

Artist in White

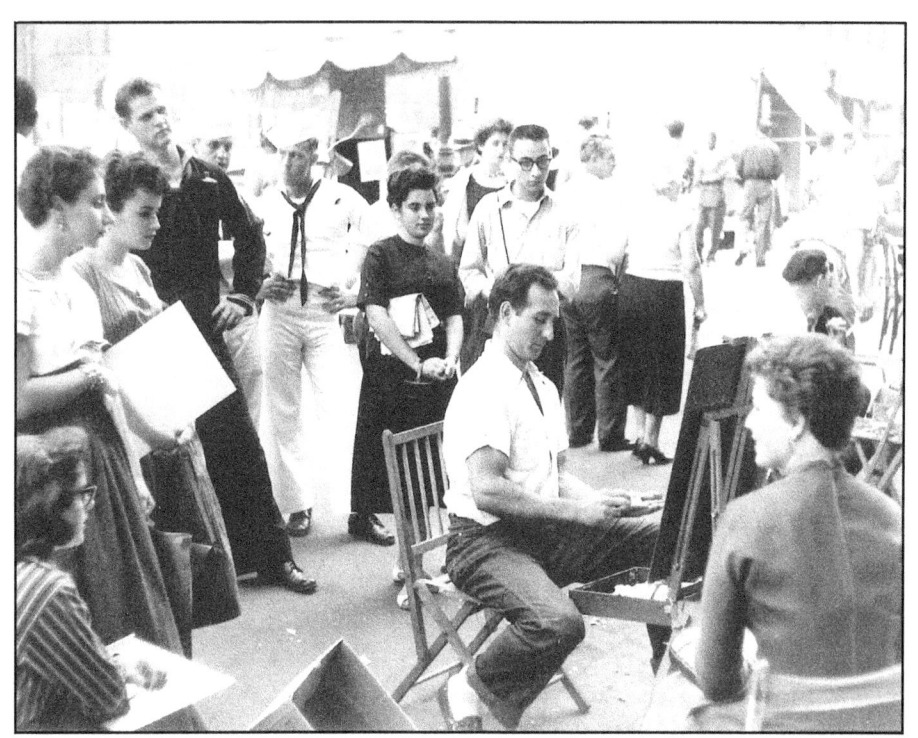

Greenwich Village Art Scene

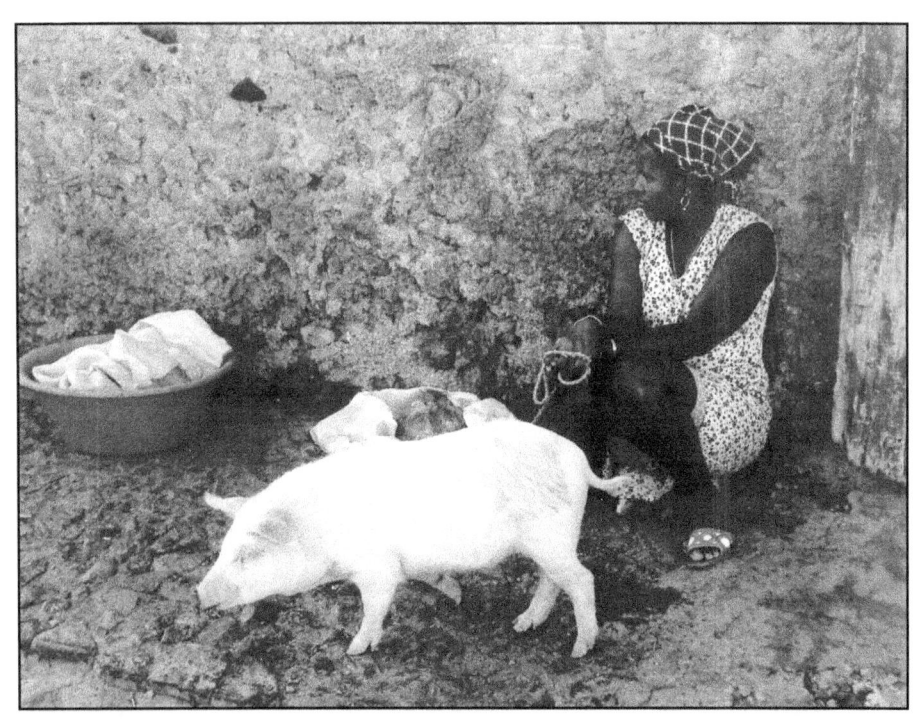

Pig for Sale

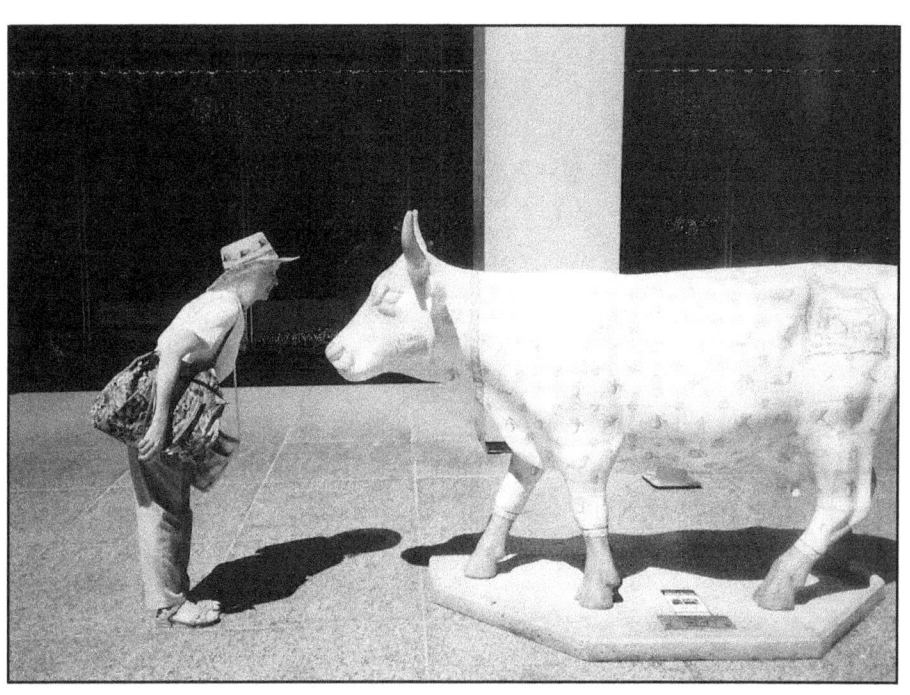

Lady Meets Cow

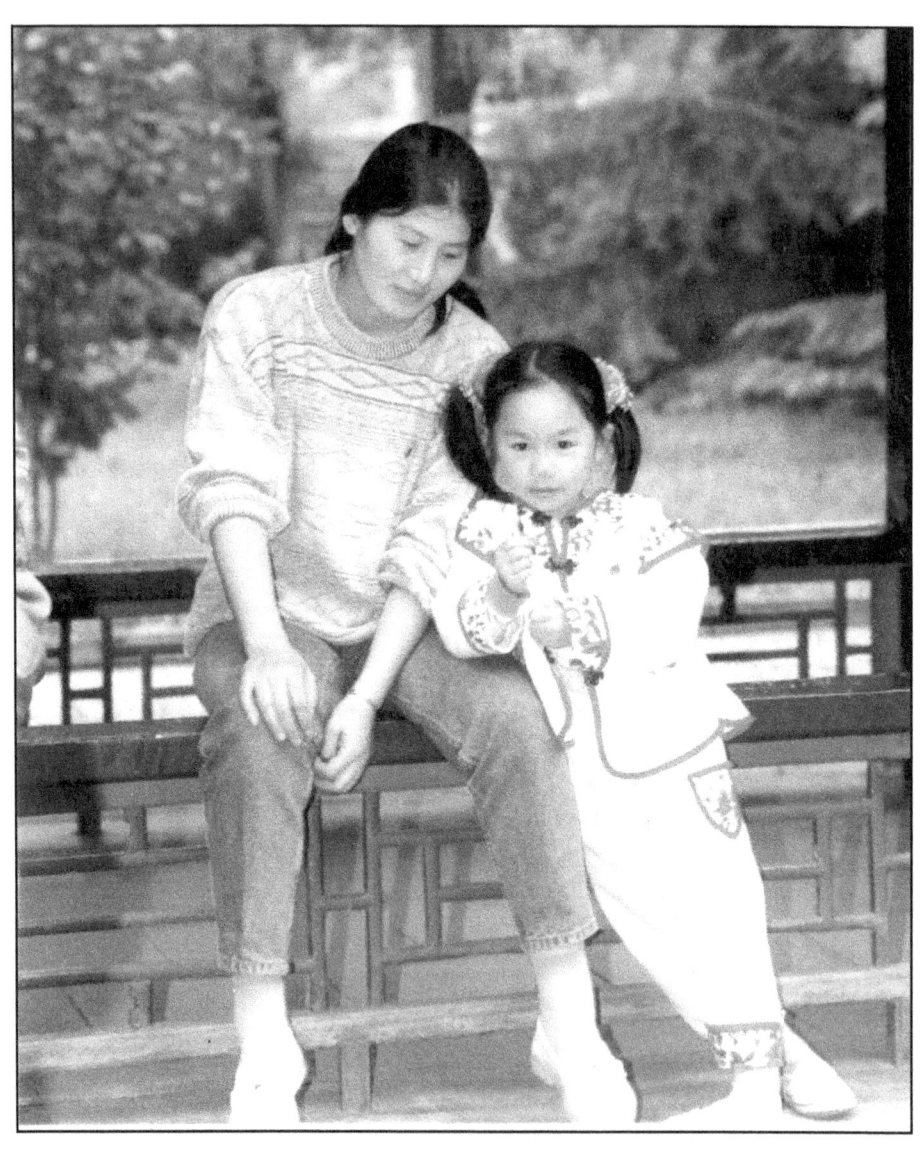

Mother & Child, Beijing

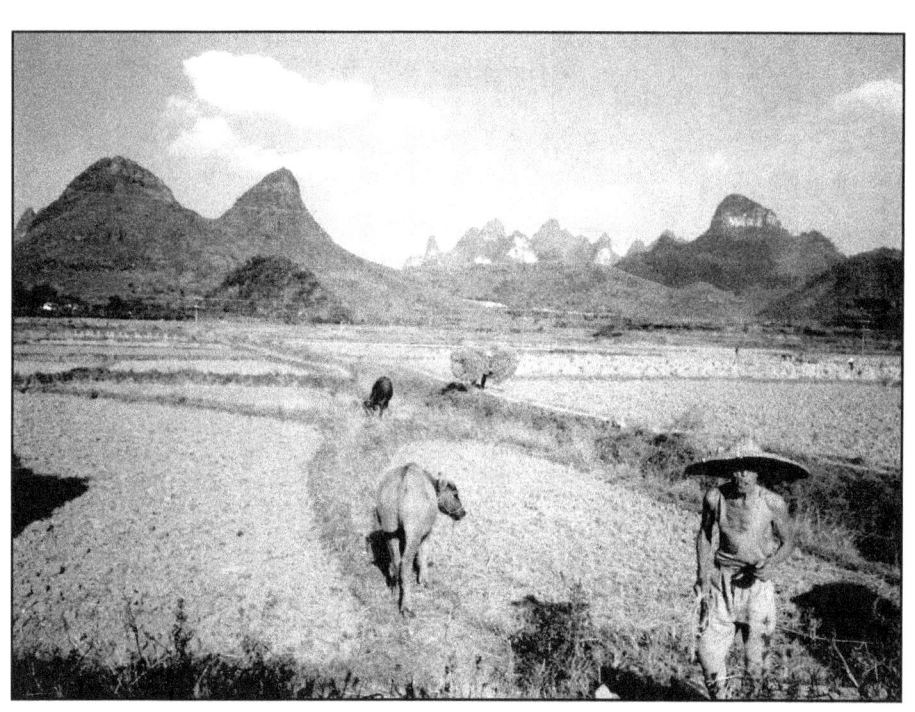

Rice Harvest, China

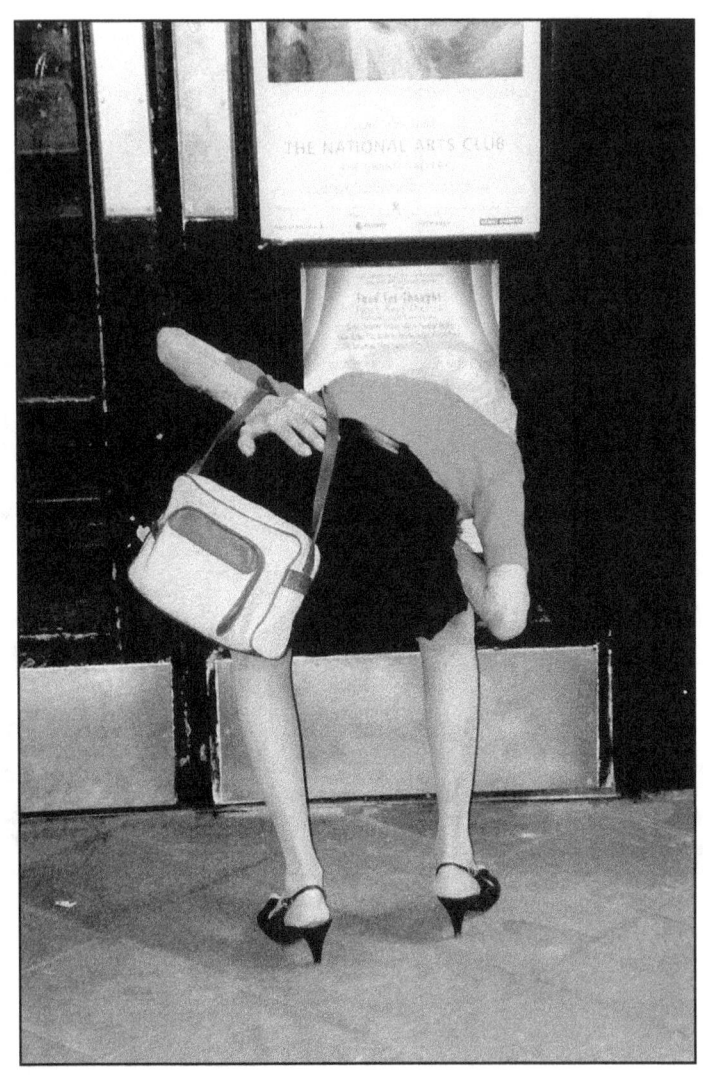

She Stoops to Peruse

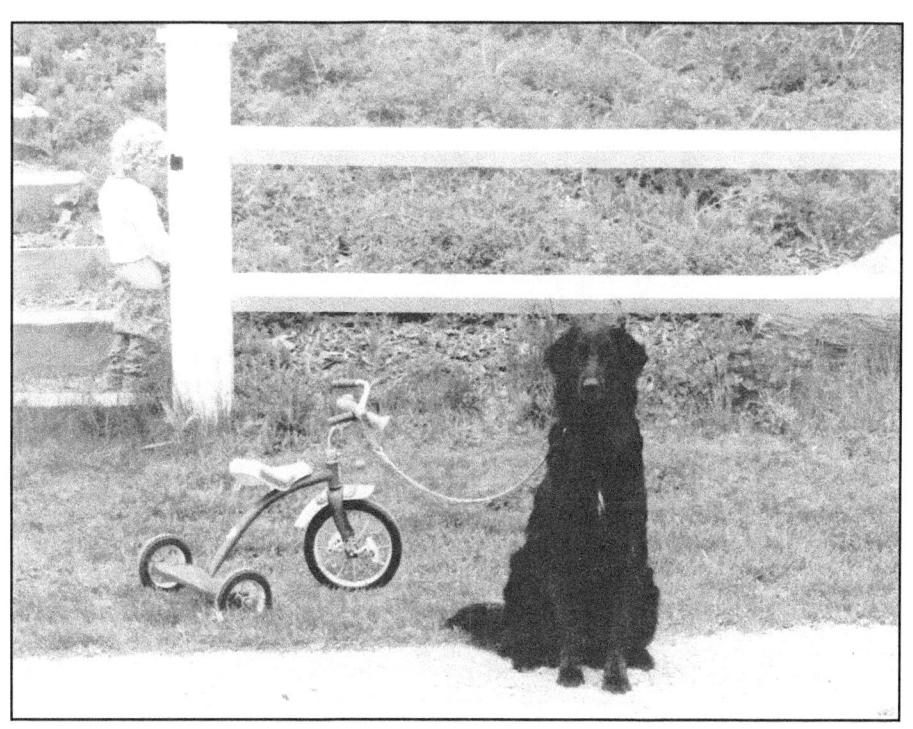

Parked Dog

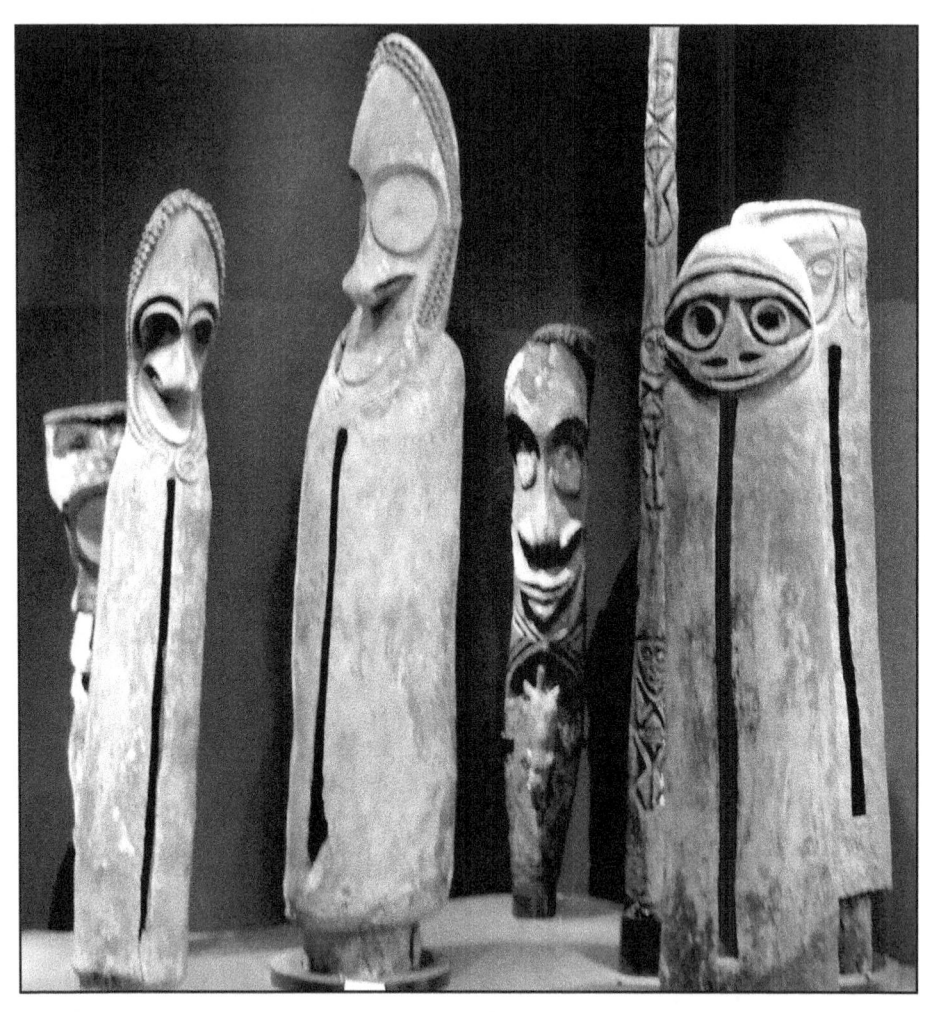

Melanesian Figures, Quai Branley, Paris

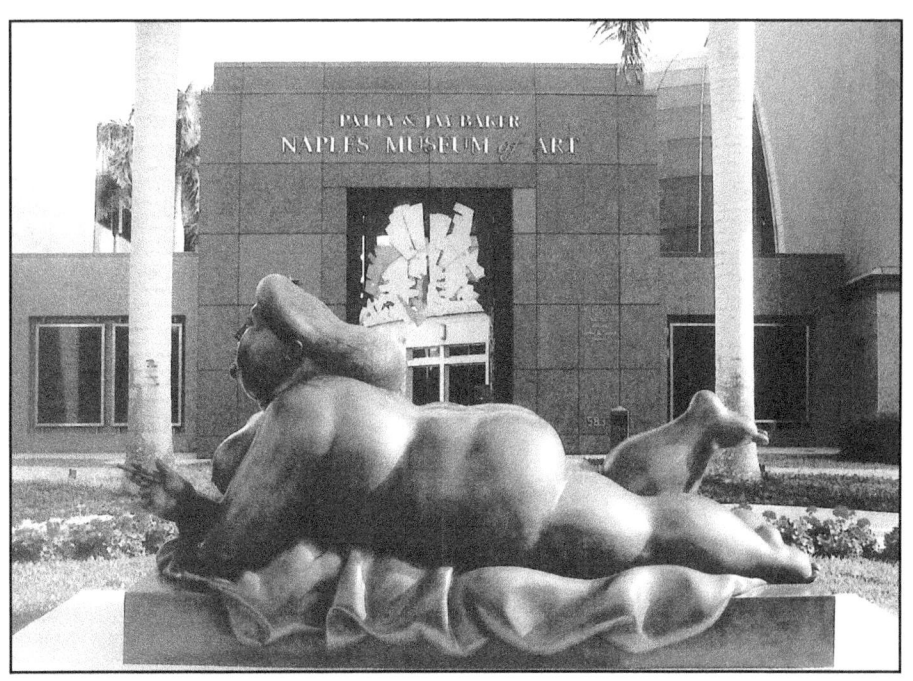

Botero Woman

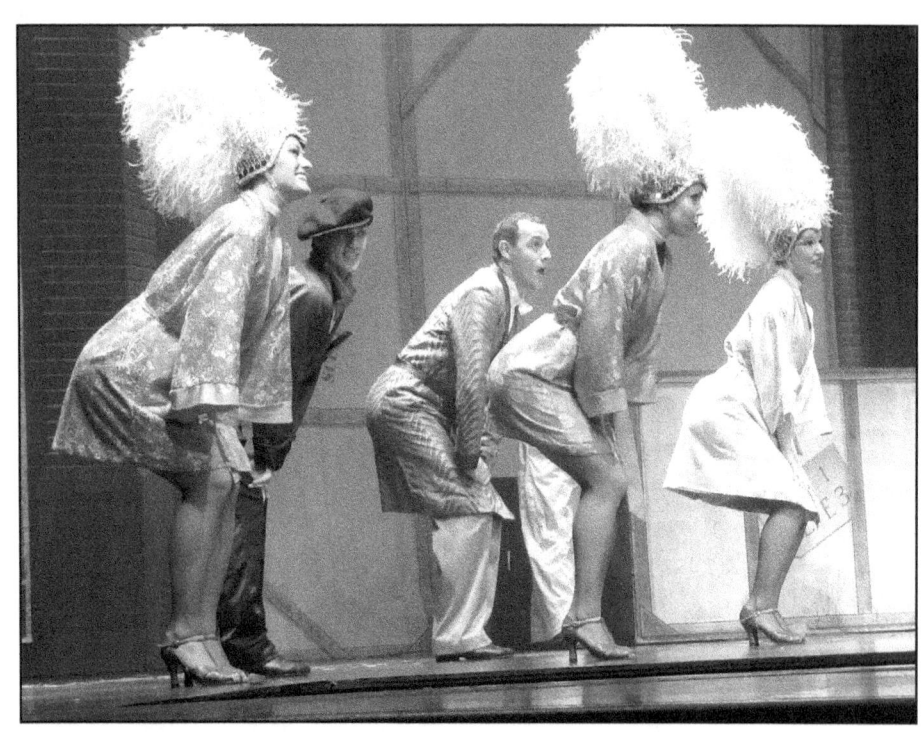

Cruise-ship Show

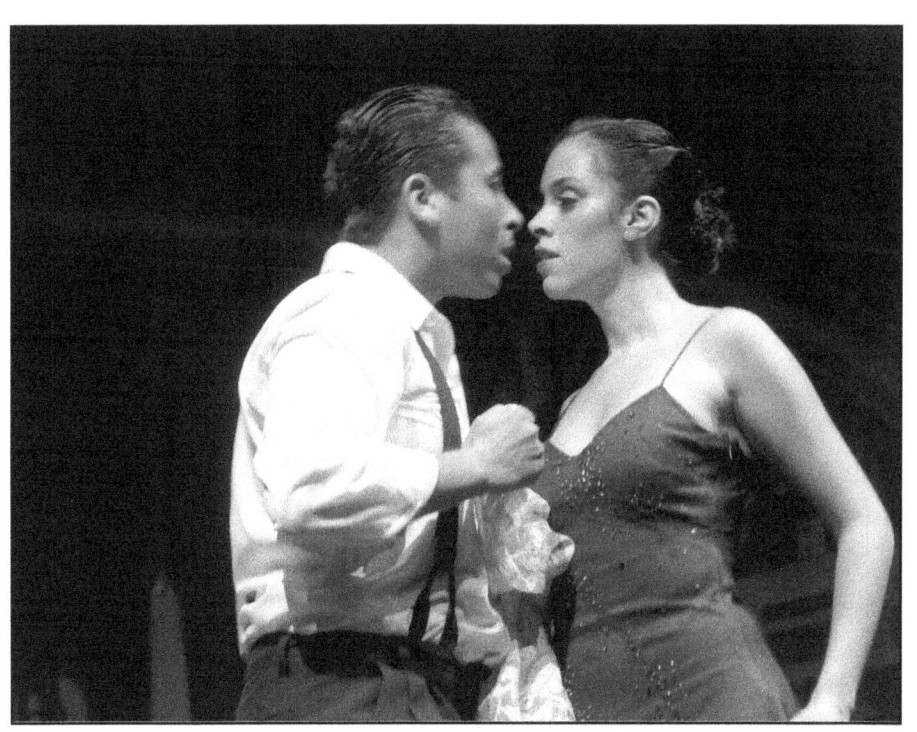

Sultry Dancers

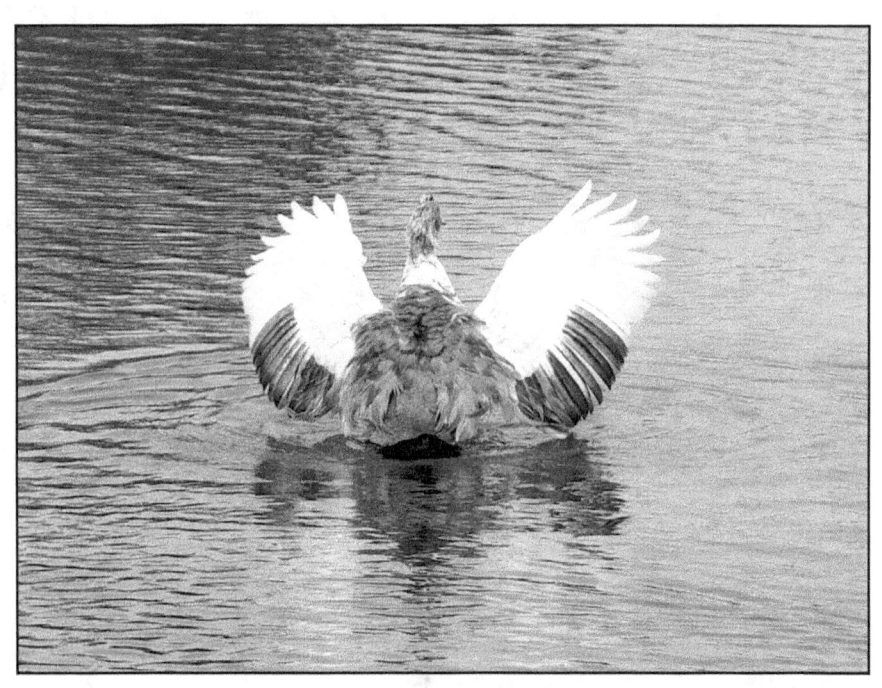

Wingspread

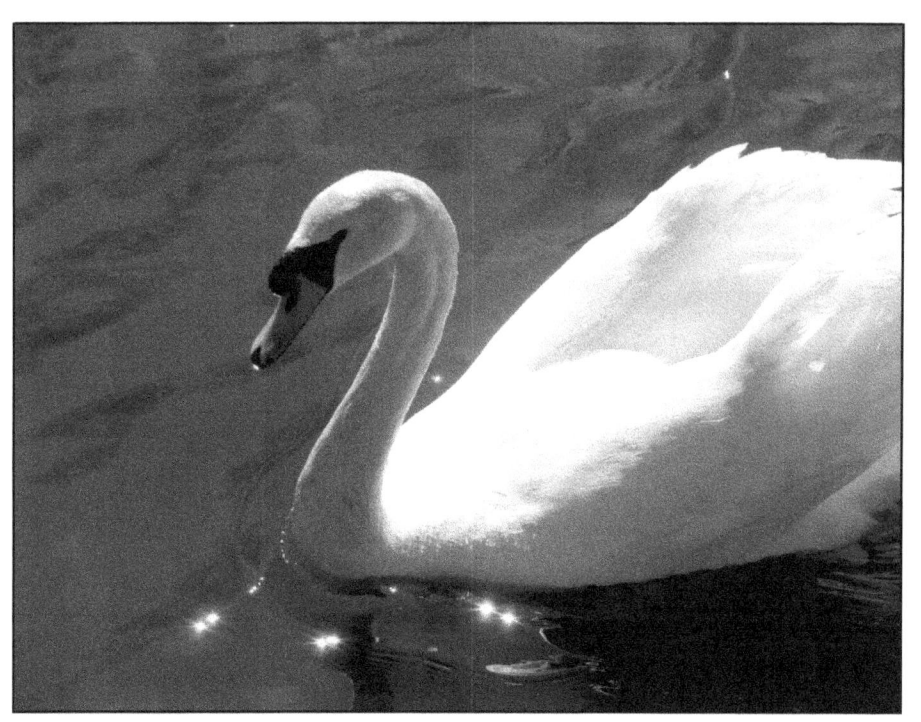

Swan

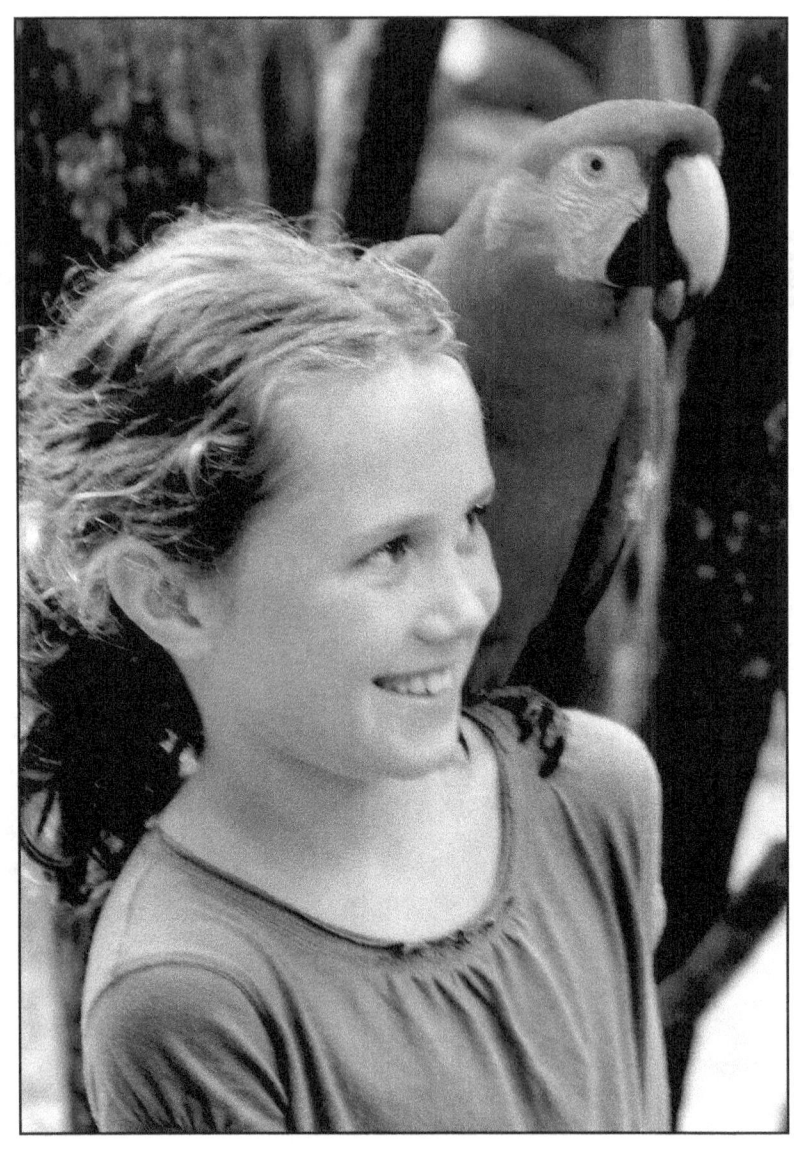

Girl and Parrot

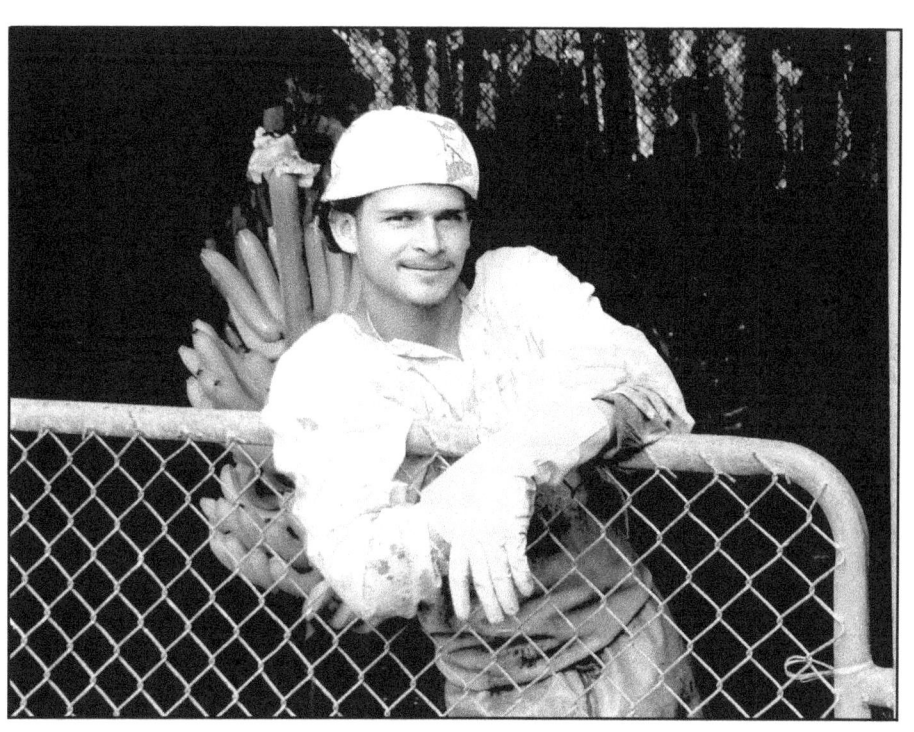

Young Banana Worker

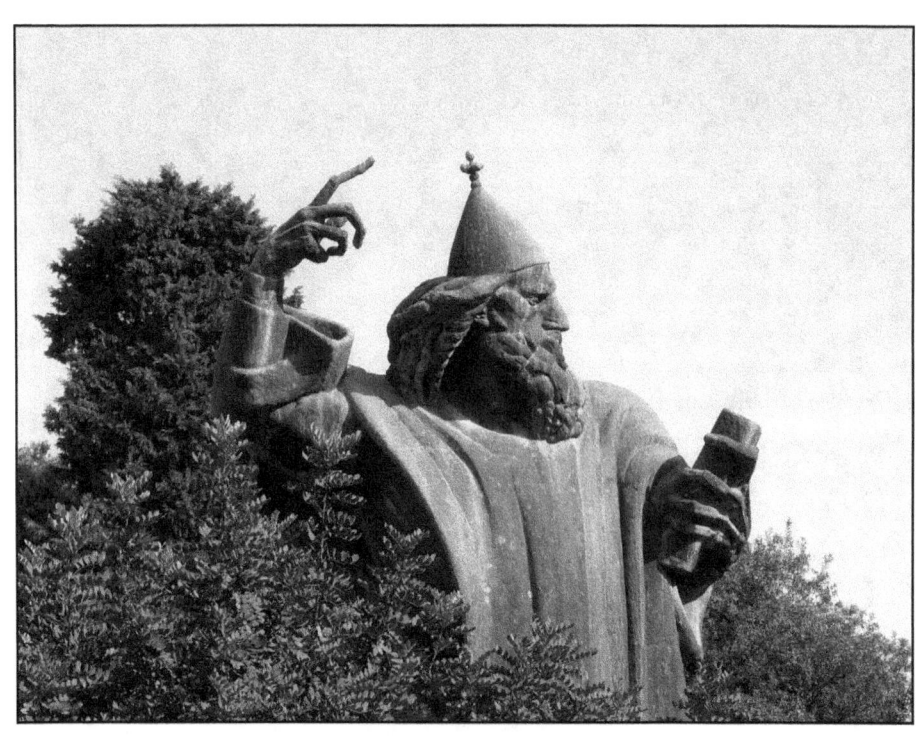

Fiery Bishop

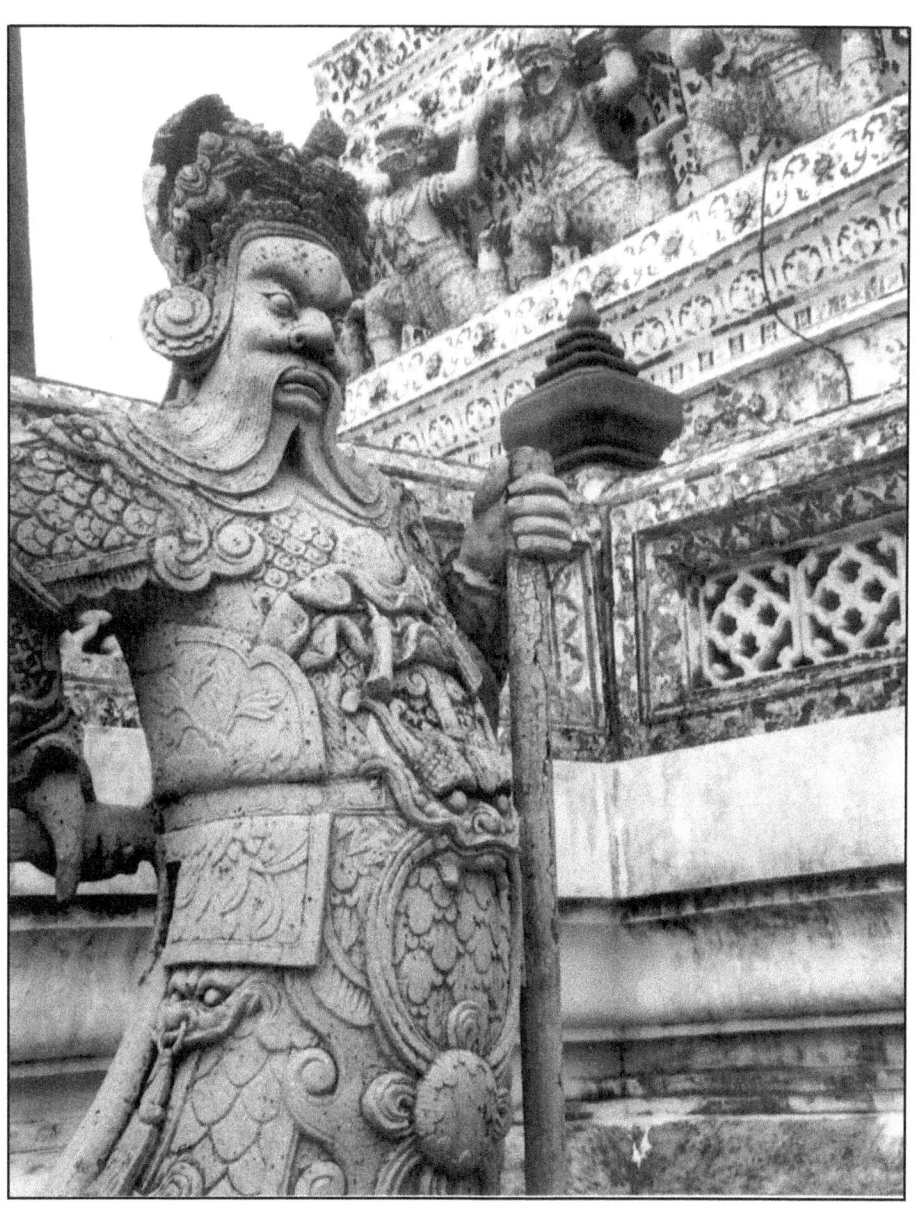

Guardian statue

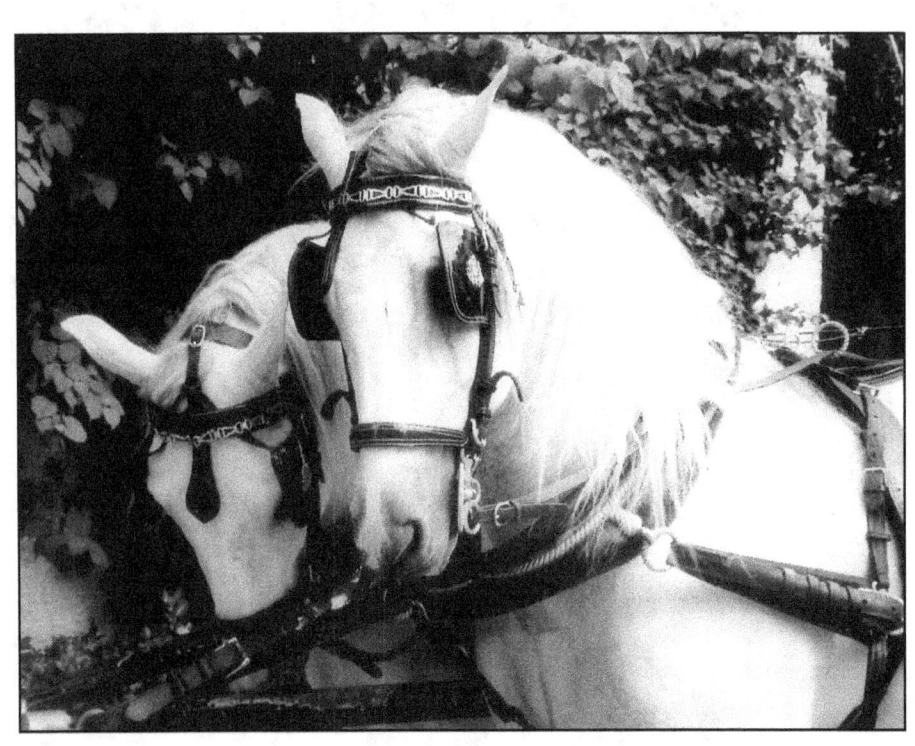

Regal Horses

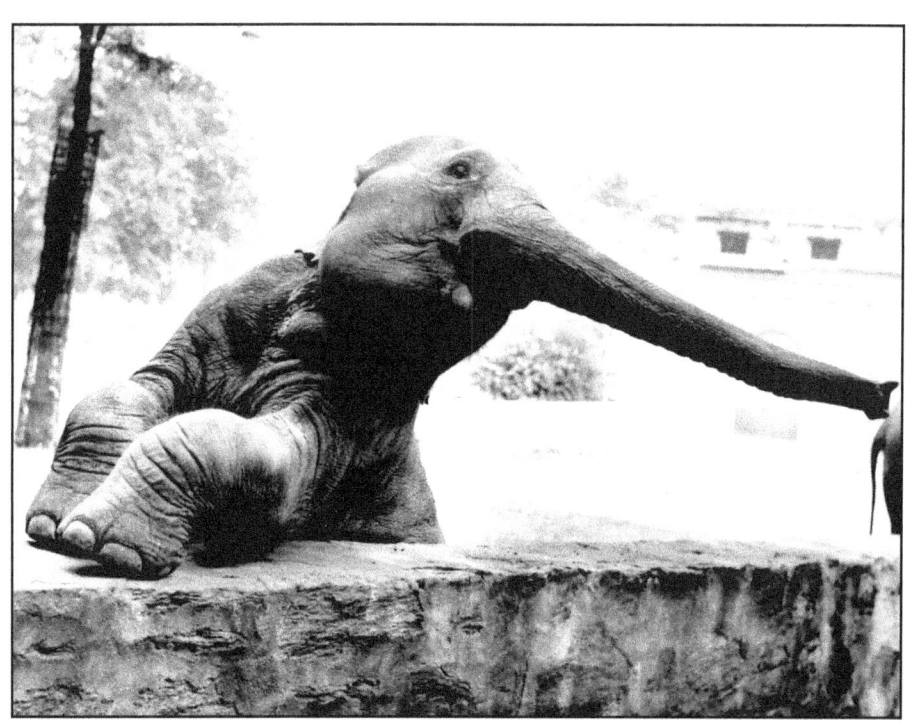

Elephant Dance

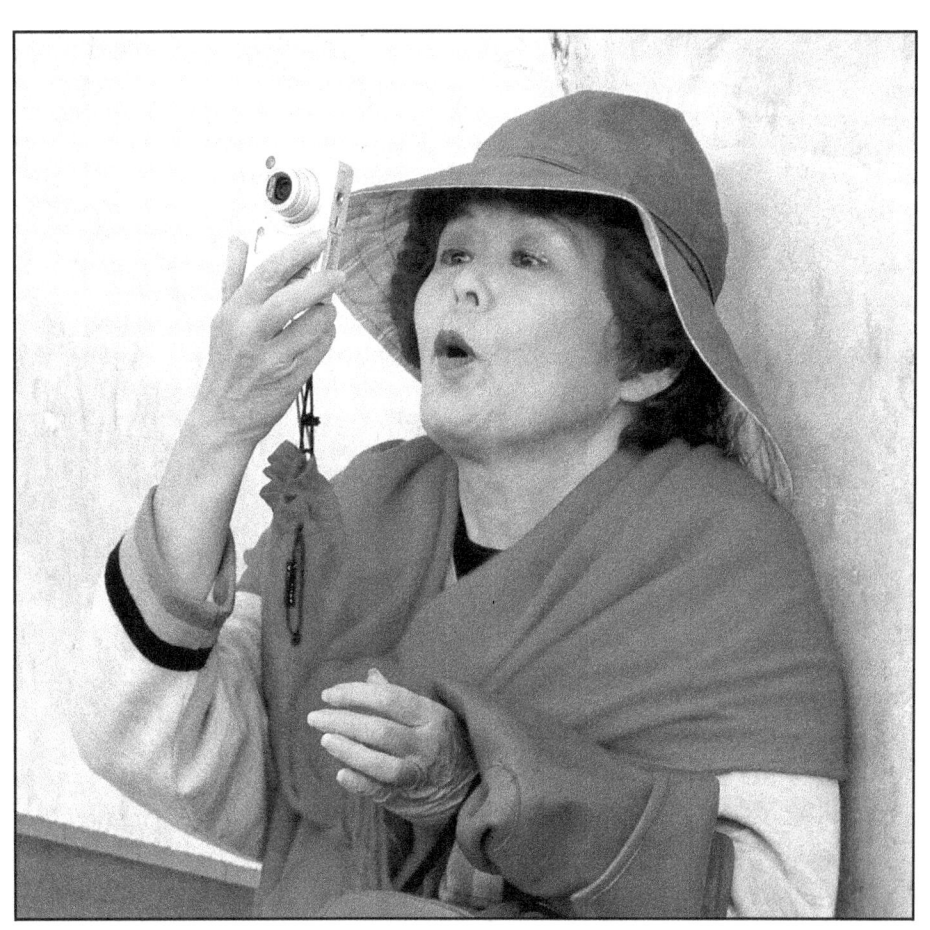

Fervent Photographer

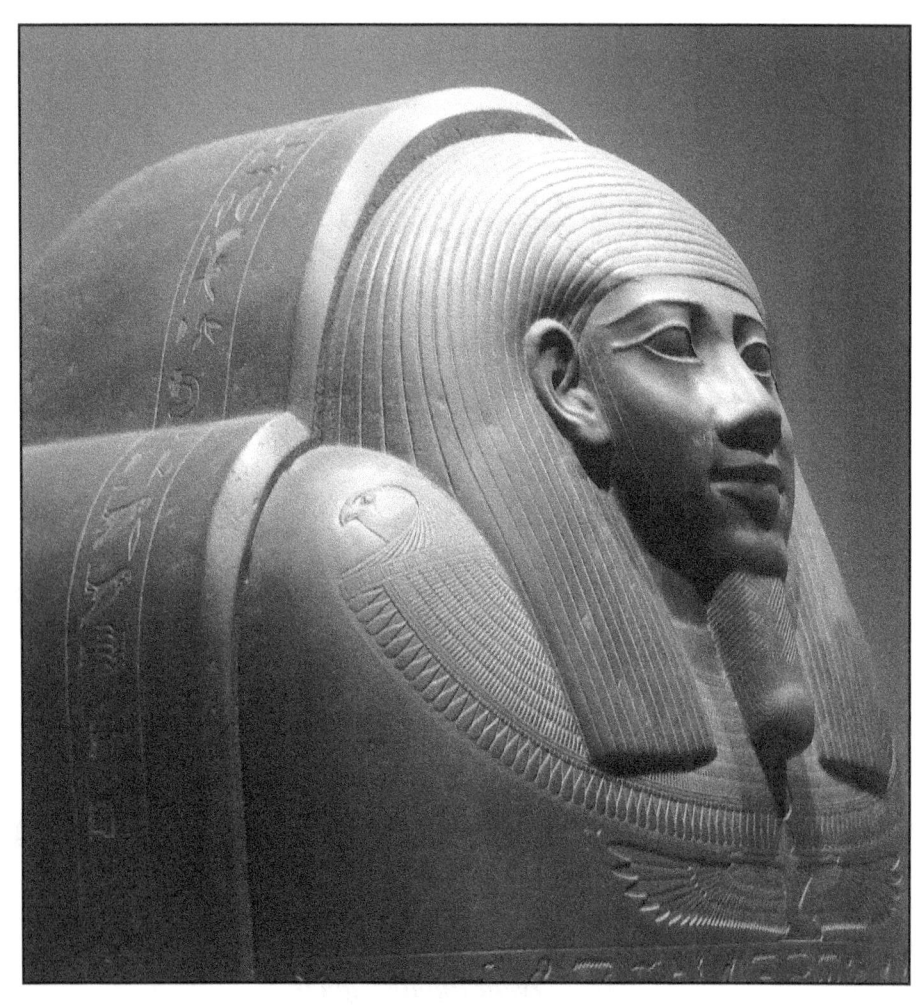

Sarcophogus

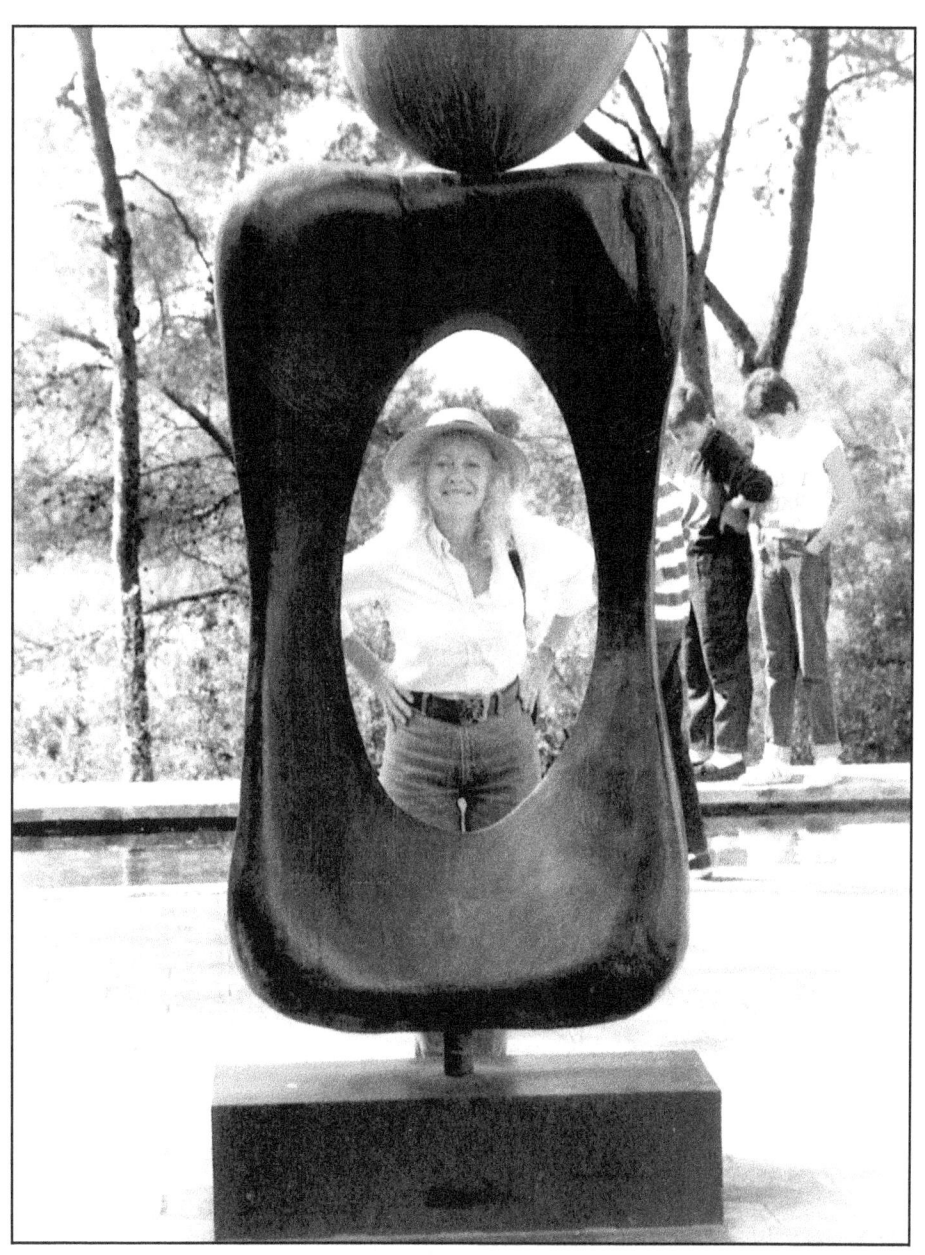

See-Through Sculpture

Bio of the Author

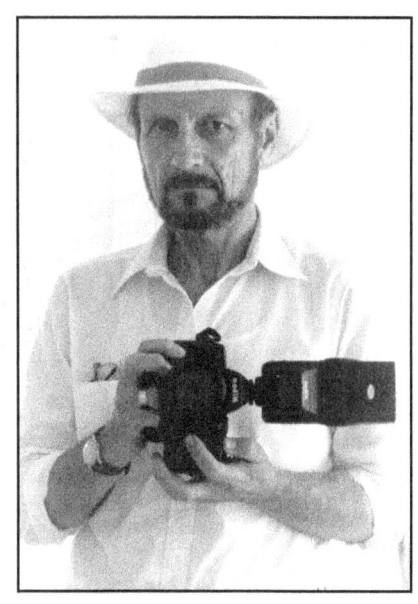

Wyn is the pseudonym for Irwin Shishko, a quixotic old fellow and a master of the art of dabbling. His wife describes him as a Renaissance Man with a small "r". An economist in his early incarnation, Wyn spent many years as a consultant to leading firms and governments, and later as VP Chief Economist of an international trading company. Following early retirement from the business world, Wyn was Chairman of a non-profit group promoting medical research, a student at the Parson's School of Design, an amateur architect who designed and built a half dozen unique homes, an avid photographer who exhibited his photos at Artworks in Richmond. Wyn has written two historical plays, and a third one, soon to be published about Mark Twain and the Devil. And when he isn't otherwise engaged, he writes poems like the luminous ones in this collection.

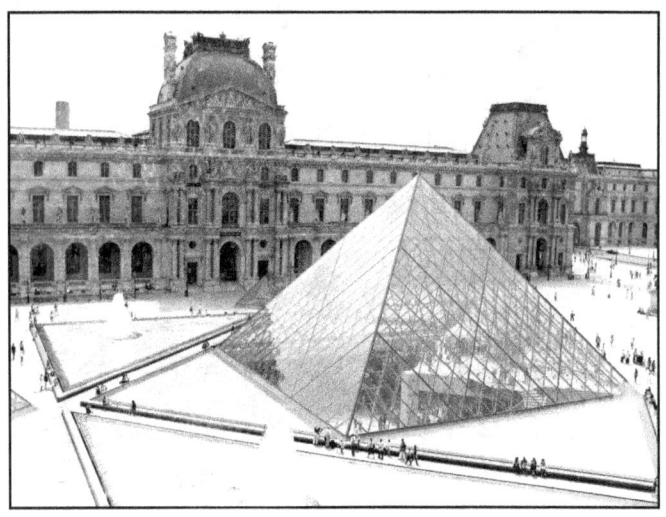

Louvre Pyramid, Paris

www.ingramcontent.com/pod-product-compliance
Lightning Source LLC
Chambersburg PA
CBHW071236170526
45165CB00003B/1113